"Startling Fact #1: Thousands, yes thousands, of people right around you are quietly hoping someone will talk to them about spiritual matters, and especially about Jesus!

"Startling Fact #2: You can be that someone! You don't have to have the gift of evangelism, and you don't need witnessing gimmicks. Walter Bleecker can show you how to do it naturally, unembarrassedly, but effectively. Read this book and try it. Your life will never be the same again."

Ray Stedman
Pastor, Peninsula Bible Church
Palo Alto, California

"Here is a book which is brilliant in its simplicity and practicality. Walter's book is readable, to the point, helpful and powerfully motivating. Our churches need what he has to say . . . Thanks, Walter, for clearing up muddled thinking."

Edward Hayes, Ph.D.
Executive Director, Mt. Hermon Association

"This book has helped me. If you are looking for techniques for non-confrontive harvesting, it will help you."

Bob Ricker
President, Baptist General Conference

"After ten years in the trenches of trying to equip the saints for works of service, I have been convinced over the past seven years that Walter Bleecker's harvesting approach is a very usable plan . . . I have personally led many people to Christ, my staff has as well, and our congregation has adopted it as our way of sharing Christ with those who are spiritually receptive."

Gene Heacock
Pastor, First Baptist Church
Foxboro, Massachusetts

"Walter Bleecker has developed what is for me a more comfortable way of talking about Jesus with friends and acquaintances. I'm a pastor and I like it better than any other pattern I have seen. And better than anything I have devised on my own."

Dr. Marvin D. Webster
Pastor, University Baptist Church
Santa Cruz, California

"I have used Walter Bleecker's harvesting tools many times and have seen people come to the Lord in many different situations: in homes, in the hospital, on an airplane, on the telephone, etc. They have included the vice president of an international insurance company and a logger."

Henry Paasonen
Pastor, Westside Alliance Church
Olympia, Washington

"Harvesting is not friendship evangelism, nor is it the work of the evangelist who has the spiritual gift. It is the practical day-to-day sharing of our faith. This is a method I can use!"

Lon Allison
Pastor/Teacher, Hope Center Covenant Church
Pleasant Hill, California

"The simplicity of the approach will blow the majority of people away, but it has to be that simple, since the Lord expected every believer to get involved in harvesting for Him. I'm anxious for the book to come out!"

Dale Flynn
Regional Director, Word of Life

"An excellent tool for the Christian who may feel inadequate or one who has limited or no knowledge of the steps to lead someone to Christ. I believe that any Christian could use this program to effectively lead people to Christ. I plan to use it in my local church."

Floyd A. Hughes
Pastor, Madison Avenue Church of the Nazarene
Carmichael, California

"In our Southern Baptist Convention we have many tools available to us. None is as clear and as easy to use as the tools Walter Bleecker uses. Our Sunday school teachers were thrilled with the easy, low-pressure approach."

Don Bloyer
Pastor, Western Hills Baptist Church
San Mateo, California

"Too many of the approaches to sharing the gospel are inflexible, 'canned,' impersonal, inhibited and limited. The method that Walter Bleecker describes to us, however, does not have those deficiencies. We found it to be very flexible, adaptable, natural and personal. Many of our people have put this training to use and are at ease with the approach."

George Lawrence
Pastor, The Free Methodist Church
Santa Cruz, California

*The
Non-Confronter's
Guide to*

LEADING A PERSON TO CHRIST

Walter S. Bleecker
with Jan Bishop

Here's Life Publishers

First Printing, March 1990
Second Printing, July 1990

Published by
HERE'S LIFE PUBLISHERS, INC.
P. O. Box 1576
San Bernardino, CA 92402

Library of Congress Cataloging-in-Publication Data
Bleecker, Walter.
    The non-confronter's guide to leading a person to Christ / Walter Bleecker.
    p.   cm.
    ISBN 0-89840-273-5
    1. Witness bearing (Christianity).   2. Evangelistic work.   I Title.
II. Title: Non-confronter's guide to leading a person to Christ.
    BV4520.B515   1990
    266 – dc20   89-27609
    CIP

Unless otherwise indicated, Scripture quotations from *The New American Standard Bible,* © The Lockman Foundation 1960, 1962, 1963, 1968, 1971, 1972, 1975, 1977.

For More Information, Write:
L.I.F.E. – P.O. Box A399, Sydney South 2000, Australia
Campus Crusade for Christ of Canada – Box 300, Vancouver, B.C., V6C 2X3, Canada
Campus Crusade for Christ – Pearl Assurance House, 4 Temple Row, Birmingham, B2 5HG, England
Lay Institute for Evangelism – P.O. Box 8786, Auckland 3, New Zealand
Campus Crusade for Christ – P.O. Box 240, Raffles City Post Office, Singapore 9117
Great Commission Movement of Nigeria – P.O. Box 500, Jos, Plateau State Nigeria, West Africa
Campus Crusade for Christ International – Arrowhead Springs, San Bernardino, CA 92414, U.S.A.

*This book is affectionately dedicated
to my wife—*

*And the many other faithful prayer warriors
from Walnut Creek who have been with me
from the beginning of this ministry and who have
loved, supported and encouraged me.*

Acknowledgments

As I have glanced at the accolades in the front of other books, I have wondered if they might not be exaggerated. Never again!

It is impossible for me to adequately thank the many dear people who have so wonderfully assisted this first time author. No doubt, God has some extra eternal blessings in store for those who have assisted me in communicating the things that surely have eternal consequences:

Norma — who loved me enough to type, type and then type some more!

Jan — for her talent, discernment and astute initial editing.

Amy and Isabel — for their extra-special prayers.

Elaine and Jacque — who over the years gave their practical advice and encouragement.

Bob — who, at my own request, patiently and lovingly forces me to say what I *really* want to say.

John — for his constant concern, and the use of his talents and facilities.

The Survivors — for being there!

Red and Gene — who typify the hundreds of pastors who have encouraged me by demonstrating how to forge ahead with prayerful enthusiasm and optimism.

Moe — a tower of strength, faithful board member and constant harvester who didn't live quite long enough to get the promised "first copy."

Contents

Foreword 8

Preface 9

A Personal Note From the Author 11

1. The Laborers Are FEW 13

2. From Self-Employed to God-Employed . . . 25

3. "Man to Man" 37

4. Learning to Labor Together 42

5. Harvesting: Non-Confrontive Evangelism . 51

6. BAAAA 63

7. A Transferable Tool 67

8. Stall and Objections 77

9. Practice Makes Permanent 88

10. Ripe Fruit or Rotten? 102

11. Community Harvesting 116

12. The Harvest Is Plentiful 129

Appendix A: Four Articles 134

Appendix B: Beginning Bible Study 142

Appendix C: The Harvesting Game 146

Appendix D: Let the Harvest Happen 157

Foreword

Over a period of ten years, I have pastored two wonderful Bible-believing churches: one in an inner-city in the San Francisco area and the other in Paso Robles, California, a small town of 10,000. Because of my great interest in evangelism, I gladly allowed the author to use me and my two churches as evangelism guinea pigs for a period of about seven years.

I can assure you that evangelistic outreach has not been easy. Over the years, with a lot of hard work, we've seen some exciting and glorious results and some heartbreaking disappointments. Nevertheless, I have found the "harvesting" methods in this book to work *effectively* in all types of circumstances. Many of the men and women in these churches have adopted this harvesting approach as a way of life! These people are for the most part *not* those who have the gift of evangelism, but they are those faithful Christians the book calls "90 percenters."

Because of my "10 percenter" mindset, it took the best part of seven years for Walter to help me convince myself that we cannot and should not try to convert 100 percent of our people into aggressive, soul-winning evangelists. I'm now convinced that we can, should and must equip 90 percenters to become fruitful harvesters.

So put away your bias and let Walter convince you too!

Pastor Leslie "Red" Ensley
First Baptist Church
Paso Robles, California

Preface

By Dr. Frances W. Grubbs
President, Simpson College

To His little band of followers relaxing at Caesarea Phillippi, Jesus had declared, "I will build My Church, and the gates of hell shall not prevail against it." In the upper room following His last supper with them, He addressed their fears by extending the hope of His return and then promised them: "Greater things will you do than I have done . . . " and still later in the garden prayed, "Father, as you sent Me into the world, I have sent them into the world."

Hence, Jesus committed to His followers, His church, the extension and completion of His own mission, which He had previously stated: "For the Son of Man is come to seek and to save that which was lost."

Following His resurrection, Jesus summarized these plans and commands into one succinct commission, which, stated in our contemporary idiom, commands: *As you go into the world, make disciples.* This commission was not vested in church leadership. It was the commission to every follower who named the name of Jesus.

For about seventeen centuries the church has distorted this command. First, we have inverted the strategy from a "go" to a "come" structure. Second, we have dissipated our resources by assuming that only a few members of the body of Christ were enabled to "make disciples."

Mr. Bleecker, through his Harvesting Seminars, is giving to the church an enabling tool to unleash the great untapped resource for community evangelism. Some have suggested that only about 10 percent of the church is gifted for evangelism. Yet the commands of Christ extend to the other 90 percent as well. Mr. Bleecker is presenting a concept and a tool to equip the other 90 percent to effectively obey Christ that as they go, they too can make disciples.

While I was the National Director of Church Growth for the Christian and Missionary Alliance, I personally worked with Mr. Bleecker in training several hundred people across the country in Harvesting Seminars. The clarity of the concept and the simplicity of the methodology was highly accepted by many who did not consider themselves gifted for personal evangelism. Furthermore, the immediate application and results by many who had never previously led another person to Christ were convincing and encouraging.

Other forgotten truths and commands that Jesus gave to His church have, at a given point in church history, been rediscovered to change the course of the church and the history of the world. This was true in the rediscovery of the great reformation doctrines in the sixteenth century. It was also true of the retrieval of the Great Commission truths in the seventeenth and eighteenth centuries that led to the modern missionary movement. It was even true of the rediscovery of truths about the Holy Spirit on the threshold of our own century. If the church will now recover the biblical concept of outreach evangelism and equip each believer to become a harvester in the whitened harvest field of his own Jeruselem, the completion of Christ's Great Commission can be completed in a single generation.

A Personal Note From the Author

My earthly father passed on a great legacy to me. He taught me to enjoy fishing! For me, fishing is a very relaxing, challenging and rewarding activity. I love to do it.

At age forty-five, my heavenly Father called me out of the business community into the ministry. He called me to become a "fisher of men" and join the ranks of some better known fishermen — those whom Jesus called personally while here on earth. Four of the twelve disciples were fishermen. Some think Jesus called fishermen because of their great persistence and patience — traits that are necessary to fish for both fish and men. It is comforting for me to know that God called and used these men who, like myself, had no seminary training.

I certainly want to be like these men who immediately followed Jesus and dedicated their lives to telling others about their Savior and Lord. It is also my desire to have the transparency of Peter, the love of John, the genuine concern of Andrew and the good judgment of James.

Anyone reading a "how to" book is certainly justified in asking, "What makes the author qualified to write it?" My number one qualification is that for many years I have worked "on the job" (at churches throughout the country) equipping others to do evangelism. God has allowed me to specialize and work exclusively in this sensitive area of church ministry. You'll find that this is not a "scholarly work" but a very practical book.

After talking to more than a thousand pastors, I know about the many frustrations pastors go through in the area of evangelistic outreach. I have been privileged to spend 100 percent of my ministerial time studying and working in this troubled area of ministry. Much of this time has been devoted to trying to find out why church members are not doing fruitful one-on-one evangelism.

I do not claim to be an expert in this area but I definitely have become a specialist in what *not* to do. In a real sense, these negative experiences have caused me to find a way to equip *every* Christian to do the natural work of joyfully harvesting as a way of life.

Every Christian *can* personally bring others to the saving knowledge of Jesus Christ. It is the church's responsibility to equip each Christian to do it. If God said do it, it must be do-able.

O·N·E

The Laborers
Are FEW

The harvest is plentiful but the laborers are few.
—Luke 10:2

The atmosphere was relaxed. Twenty pastors representing various denominations were discussing their personal evangelism experiences. The question before them was straightforward: "What has been your experience in equipping others to do evangelistic outreach in your church?"

The pastor of a Baptist church said, "We have tried "Evangelism Explosion." It's really a great program, but, at our church, our people didn't sustain their initial enthusiasm."

Having recently completed the "Evangelism Explosion" training, I immediately wanted to question this pastor further but waited as other pastors revealed even more startling experiences.

An associate pastor from the largest Covenant church in the area said, "Well, we've tried to use the Campus Crusade training several times. It did some good but we gave it up."

I wanted to jump in and say, "Why in the world did you give it up?" Someone from Campus Crusade for Christ had led my wife and me to Jesus and eventually my whole family made a commitment. Yes, I wanted to stand in defense of both Dr. James Kennedy and Dr. Bill Bright, who, in my opinion, have done more to help the local church do evangelism than any other men in all of Christendom. Instead, I sat in silence.

"Our experience has been similar," said the pastor of a Presbyterian church.

As the rest of the pastors shared, the pattern became obvious. Every pastor in the room had similar experiences. They all had experimented with various approaches. Every program eventually had run its course and stopped.

The moderator, a senior pastor of a multi-thousand membership evangelical church, made a startling statement: "I have been asking the same question for years and the answer is always the same. My conclusion is that all programs fail."

Now, quite frankly, that is my kind of statement. I like folks who don't beat around the bush. But this statement shook me to the core, and I still haven't gotten over it. It confirmed an equally bold statement made by Dr. Peter Wagner, who is a well-known church growth spokesman: "Collective Christian wisdom as well as actual field research has shown that nothing we have done in the past has been able to sustain vigorous and continuous evangelism."

My whole being cried out, *Why?* If programs are 100 percent Christ-centered, if they are solidly based on Scripture, if they are executed by enthusiastic Christians who are led by the Holy Spirit and steeped in prayer, *What is wrong?* Why do these excellent programs, administered by godly men and women, eventually fail in the local churches? Why is it that evangelism is such a sensitive, touchy area of ministry? Why is it that when we just mention the word *evangelism* most people have negative responses?

The Fields Are Ripe

Since you picked up this book and have read this far, it is probably safe to assume you are more than casually interested in reaching non-Christians with the gospel.

Let me stop right here and tell you what is ahead. This book uncovers the appalling fact that over 90 percent of evangelical Christians have never purposefully led even one person to the saving knowledge of Jesus Christ. It reveals how every believer can share in this joy by reaching out to others in a way that is natural and non-confrontive. And it presents detailed steps for churches to follow to equip their leaders so they, in turn, can train each member.

This book introduces the concept of *harvesting* — evangelism for non-confronters. *Harvesting* is the act of leading those whom God has prepared to Him and encouraging everyone else.

The major fallacy that must be dispelled is that unbelievers are not open and receptive to the gospel message. Today people are more willing than ever to talk about spiritual things. Christian scholars like Francis Schaeffer have said this for years, and now, after his death, even secular humanists are beginning to agree with him. People are flocking to join cultish groups in unprecedented numbers. Perhaps there never has been a time in human history when people are more willing and open to not only talk about spiritual things but also to take action.

This truth seems more obvious than ever:

Behold, I say to you, lift up your eyes, and look on
the fields, that they are white for *harvest* (John 4:35).

We are surrounded by willing and ready *pre-Christians.* A pre-Christian is one who seems to be open to
spiritual things and has not rejected Jesus Christ as Lord.
The sad thing is they don't know they are ready and we
have conditioned ourselves to believe they are not. We have
made ourselves content to leave our pre-Christian friends
and relatives in an unsaved, uninformed state until they
die and enter into a new phase of unnecessary suffering for
eternity.

Bill Bright, the dynamic founder of Campus
Crusade for Christ, claims statistics show that one out of
four non-Christians in this country is ready to make a commitment to Jesus Christ. One-fourth of the people out there
would come to Christ if someone would just explain the
gospel to them. This is more than *30 million people.*

Perhaps some think Dr. Bright is overly optimistic.
However, whether we consider the possibility to be one out
of five, six or seven, the numbers are still overwhelming.

To make Dr. Bright's figures even more meaningful, consider the attendance at a public event or sports
activity: Every fourth person we see is ready to come to
Christ. Picture our over-crowded highways: Every fourth
car on the road carries a non-Christian ready to make a
commitment to Christ. Walk into a store or restaurant any
time, anywhere: Every fourth person we see is receptive
and willing to come to Christ. In all probability, these
people at the public events, on the roads and in the stores
and restaurants will be face to face with a born-again Christian sometime within any given week. The sad thing is that
these two people, the Christian and the pre-Christian, will
happily talk about everything imaginable except the one
thing that is the most important — a personal relationship

with Jesus Christ. *Why?*

We know God has faithfully done His work — many are "white for harvest." He has faithfully prepared millions of people to come to Himself. And, as if God's Word needed help, in our Christian bookstores there are shelves of how-to books on every method of evangelism imaginable. In addition, evangelical ministers welcome the opportunity to talk about how to communicate the gospel. There is neither a shortage of materials nor advice on leading people to the saving knowledge of Jesus Christ.

The Root of the Problem

The real problem is the vast majority of us don't think in terms of purposefully letting receptive, willing pre-Christians respond to the wonderful gospel message. The Gospel of Luke confirms this: "The harvest is plentiful, but the laborers are few" (Luke 10:2).

I've observed many healthy, active laborers in the churches of America. Most are busily involved in doing everything else *but* working in the harvest field. According to most evangelical church leaders, this describes about 90 percent of their people. One might say we have a labor problem right here in our local churches. Most dedicated church workers are not comfortable working in the area of evangelistic outreach, although they often are active in other areas. They declare, "I witness by my life," and they miss out on the joyful ministry of actively leading people to Jesus Christ.

Something seems radically wrong. Why are only 10 percent or less of the believers actively involved in sharing the good news of Christ with nonbelievers? Maybe the answer to this problem is so simple that we have missed it completely; extraordinarily complex problems sometimes are solved in ordinary ways.

The 10 Percent/90 Percent Problem

Let me describe what I call the 10 percent/90 percent problem. The 10 percent and 90 percent represent the number of believers who actively present the gospel message to non-Christians and those who do not. Ten percent of the believers (10 percenters) are very interested in evangelism and have an unusually strong desire to see everyone saved. Sharing the gospel is almost as natural to them as talking and breathing. Ninety percent of the believers (90 percenters), on the other hand, have a genuine concern for the lost but are uncomfortable with most evangelism methods. They claim to witness by their lives and seldom actively lead others to Christ.

The scenario goes something like this. When any kind of evangelism project comes up at the church, invariably the pastor asks one of the most active 10 percenters to help implement it. Frequently, it is a person who has been pressuring the leadership for more evangelism, so he or she eagerly accepts the challenge. With much enthusiasm, the 10 percenter forms a coalition with other 10 percenters. They get together and aggressively attempt to persuade 90 percenters to become involved in an exciting new program. At the same time, the 90 percenters attempt to convince the 10 percenters they already are deeply involved in other important things. Their clarion call is, "After all, evangelism isn't the only important thing going on around here." The 10 percenters counter by saying, "How are we ever to grow unless we all reach out?"

And so it goes. The scenario is all too familiar to leaders in the evangelical church. No matter how good the evangelism program, no matter how well it is publicized and promoted, it is almost impossible to involve anyone other than the 10 percenter. If, on occasion, one of the 90 percenters decides to participate, he or she drops out as soon as there is an opportunity.

Even the most active church leaders often are not personally involved in aggressive evangelism outreach. These same leaders, at the same time, insist that evangelism be one of the top priorities of the church. Have you ever wondered why? You can be reasonably sure it's because these leaders are frustrated 90 percenters.

The fact is that the 90 percenters usually will resist any kind of aggressive evangelism training. We have been trying to force them to do what most 10 percenters do naturally and the programs die because of limited involvement. It just doesn't work and it never will. In addition, forcing 90 percenters to do things that make them feel uncomfortable only causes resentment.

100 Percent Commitment

Many would, by default, advocate simply to equip the 10 percenters and let them do it all. However, the Great Commission instructs every one of us to: "Go into all the world and preach the gospel to all creation" (Mark 16:15). This is for *100 percent* of Christ's followers — not just 10 percent. In Matthew 4:19, Jesus didn't say "Follow Me and I will make 10 percent of you fishers of men." The Great Commission is meant for every Christian.

Some of you may be saying, "Well, what about the spiritual gift factor? Isn't it true that God gives many different gifts to different people so that they can work in different parts of the Body of Christ?" Yes, that is certainly true. Although God's Word doesn't say so, it is probably also true that about 10 percent are gifted lay evangelists or at least potentially gifted in the area of evangelism. That means all the rest have different gifts.

Unfortunately, in many ways we have misunderstood the biblical precepts of discovering and using our spiritual gifts to the extent that we use them as rationale for becoming specialists. We rationalize that God wants us to do just one job within the body — "Don't ask me to evangelize because it is not my spiritual gift." On the contrary, the biblical teaching is that all Christians are called, chosen and privileged to tell others the good news about Jesus Christ. It never is an option.

Jesus' first command to His disciples was:

Follow Me, and I will make you fishers of men (Matthew 4:19).

His last command was:

Go therefore and make disciples of all the nations (Matthew 28:19).

It sounds like these are very urgent concerns of the Lord. *God is not willing that any should perish.* He wants every believer to locate and let those whom He has already prepared come to Himself. That's the exciting challenge of the Great Commission and it is for *everyone.* Search the Scriptures; you will not find one verse that exempts *anyone.*

Even so, equipping members to do evangelism is one of the most troublesome areas in the church today. Tensions caused by discussing evangelism run from feelings of intense emotion to complete indifference. The primary issue is not the program, which everyone agrees should be scriptural, but rather what happens when one group pushes to get the other group to be more aggressive. The group of 10 percenters believes aggression is necessary for better results while the group of 90 percenters points out, and rightly so, that being too aggressive can do more harm than good. Round and round they go.

In order to get a better grasp of what actually is happening in the local church, we need to take a much closer look at these two different groups. The difference between the two groups will shed invaluable light on the problem.

A 10 Percenter Is Not a 90 Percenter

In *Figure 1*, the church is separated into two groups. On the left are "confronters" and on the right are "non-confronters."

An Overall Look at the Membership of the Average Evangelical Church

Confronters – 10 Percent (10 percenters)	Non-confronters – 90 Percent (90 percenters)
Spiritually gifted lay evangelists, pastors and those called to full-time ministry.	Spiritually gifted in areas *other* than evangelism.
Those who like to or because of their calling must confront with the gospel.	Those who definitely prefer not to confront with the gospel.
Should be trained to be soul winners with Evangelism Explosion or Reaching Your World video training.	Should be trained to implement the program detailed herein.

Figure 1

The confronters are spiritually gifted as evangelists. They are natural confronters and do it with ease and great joy. Usually included in this group are the pastor and his staff and those generally referred to as "full-time Christian workers." Even if some of these identify strongly with non-confronters and have other spiritual gifts, by virtue of their calling or because of their office, they are involved in actively confronting others with the gospel. Therefore, they are automatically placed here.

On the right side of *Figure 1* we have the largest group—the non-confronters. They are spiritually gifted in

22   LEADING A PERSON TO CHRIST

a variety of areas other than evangelism. With varying degrees of intensity, they dislike confrontation. These believers rely almost solely on "witnessing with their lives" when it comes to sharing spiritual things with the unsaved.

When church members see these charts, they usually are willing to place themselves on one side or the other. It's simply a matter of personal preference. However, when considering spiritual gifts, it is dangerous to think in black and white terms. Some may be singly or multi-gifted so there are exceptions.

Figure 2 is an attempt to simplify and generalize the differences between confronters (10 percenters) and non-confronters (90 percenters), although of course you will find exceptions.

The Differences Between Confronters and Non-confronters

Confronters (10 percenters)	Non-confronters (90 percenters)
Regularly lead non-Christians to the saving knowledge of Jesus Christ.	Have never had the joy of personally leading someone to Christ but have done some things to help.
Have unusually strong desires to see everyone come to Christ.	Have a desire to see others come to Christ but are not overwhelmed by it.
Have spiritual gifts or use their God-given talents in the area of evangelism.	Have spiritual gifts but use their talents and abilities in other areas of ministry.
Love to persuade, convince and urge.	Say they witness by their lives.
Constantly look for creative ways to talk about Jesus Christ.	Seldom are comfortable with talking about spiritual things.
Use every opportunity to practice outreach.	Outreach is not foremost in their thinking.

Love to give their own personal testimony in public or private.	Uncomfortable with talking about their personal relationship with Christ.
Like to hand out tracts, do door-to-door work, visit prisons and rest homes, do rescue mission work, etc.	Keep a low profile when it comes to one-on-one evangelism.

Figure 2

Because there are people with similar personalities and temperaments in both categories, confronters and non-confronters cannot be identified by these traits alone. It is not uncommon to think that extroverts would naturally be the confronters, but this is not necessarily so. Many soft-spoken, almost shy, 10 percenters can be wonderfully aggressive and very effective confronters, and some very forward, talkative 90 percenters fit perfectly into the non-confronter group.

If it were possible to feed into a computer the personality data on both 10 percenters and 90 percenters, I believe the following three generalities would emerge.

Generality One

Ten percenters love to innovate. They like a great variety of options and will be enthusiastic about any biblical method to lead people to the Lord. They refuse to be boxed in by any one plan. Like the pilots of old, they prefer to fly by the seat of their pants.

Ninety percenters, on the other hand, would rather stay in familiar territory. They prefer friendship or lifestyle evangelism. They appreciate spiritual discussions that are non-threatening and do not like evangelism methods that might embarrass them and others.

Generality Two

The 10 percenters are intent on removing every

obstacle to a salvation commitment. They have a compulsion to create opportunities to develop dialogue so they can discuss and eventually confront.

The 90 percenters are not afraid to talk but prefer to avoid controversial subjects. Unconsciously they may even try to steer the conversation *away* from a confrontation with the gospel truth.

Generality Three

The 10 percenters love to show non-confronters how to be more aggressive. Because of their nature, 10 percenters have a desire to change 90 percenters. Being confronters, they see no reason why they should not confront the non-confronters and encourage them to be a little more like themselves.

The 90 percenters are threatened by 10 percenters (in varying degrees). They usually respect the confronter's tenacity and enthusiasm but do not want to be shown how to become more aggressive. As far as evangelism is concerned, they will not model 10 percenters.

By now you no doubt sense my frustration with what appears to be a 10 percent/90 percent stalemate. Later I will offer a solution. In the meantime, I would like you to see how my conversion experience and subsequent call to a very specialized ministry permitted this rather involved solution to slowly unfold.

T·W·O

From Self-Employed to God-Employed

Follow Me, and I will make you fishers of men.
—Matthew 4:19

I was fortunate to be raised on the east coast by a large, loving family. Attending church was a way of life.

During World War II, I spent three years in the Navy. After the war, I graduated from college and went to work for the 3M Company as a technical sales representative. Within a year I met my wife at a church picnic. She was brought up in the midwest and had a church background almost identical to my own. The church we attended is often called a "liturgical" church. We regularly recited the Creeds and over the years were exposed to readings from the Gospels, Epistles and Psalms. However, this particular denomination put no emphasis on reading the Bible and what we have since come to know as a personal relationship with Jesus Christ.

Four children later, I was transferred to the west coast by my company. My family and I became active in another church of that same denomination. One summer, a neighborhood child invited our pre-teen twin daughters

25

to attend a Bible camp at a place called *Camp Koinonia.* The child's father came by and outlined the week-long program. Although it was sponsored by a church group unfamiliar to us, it sounded excellent so we let them go. Our daughters had a delightful time and upon their return announced that they had "received Jesus Christ as their Lord and Savior and were saved." We received this jubilant message with stunned silence. Fearing our sweet little girls had been taken in by a group of religious fanatics, we waited to see what would happen. Much to our surprise, they did not try to talk us into changing churches and we got no pressure whatever from the members of the "fanatic" group.

The only obvious change in our children was that they set the alarm ahead one hour and happily got up every morning to read the Bible. We were unaware of it at the time but learned later that there was a group of forty-five people regularly praying for our daughters and their unsaved parents.

Several weeks later I was having my hair cut when out of the blue my barber said something about Jesus Christ. "Not you too!" I said and proceeded to tell him the story of my Bible-reading daughters. He got so excited he immediately stopped cutting my hair and went into the back room to get a copy of *Good News for Modern Man.*[1] He challenged me to take it home and read the Gospel of John from beginning to end. That evening I was so impressed with the common sense and clarity of John that I insisted my wife read it before going to bed.

The next day when I took the book back, he asked if we would be willing to attend a couples' conference. He assured me it would be a fun time and that practical spiritual things would be discussed.

Several weeks later we joined my barber friend and his wife at a Campus Crusade couples' meeting at Mission

Springs Conference Center in Scotts Valley, California. During this meeting, Howard Ball carefully presented The Four Spiritual Laws booklet[2] to the group in order to make the gospel message crystal clear. I'll never forget how he then skillfully converted the truths from the booklet into direct but gentle qualifying questions. To alleviate any pressure, he said, "Now please don't say yes to these questions unless you honestly and sincerely mean it." He had laid down an awesome challenge, but at the same time he gave us permission to gracefully back off without any overwhelming feelings of guilt.

What he was really saying was that the decision was 100 percent mine—not his or anyone else's. Up until now, no one had ever done this for me. I had been preached at, poked with the gospel and told that I should be born again and saved. I had also been told that I was going to hell. But no one had ever taken the time to ask me to respond honestly to these simple but urgent questions.

Howard Ball created a wonderful problem for both my wife and me. He lovingly put us in the position where we could not in good conscience say no. Because we could honestly and sincerely agree with every question he asked and because we received Jesus Christ as our Lord and Savior, Howard helped us right into the Kingdom of God. Before we knew what had happened, we were born again. For the first time in our lives we knew for certain that we had the free gift of eternal life.

I looked over at my wife; she was crying. I did not have a big emotional experience. Some do and some don't. But the amount of emotion has nothing to do with the sincerity of the commitment. What we both had and still have is a peace and joy that is impossible to explain.

Following our daughters lead, we too started reading the Bible. We both were amazed at how much easier it was to understand. Slowly and positively our lives began to change.

My first reaction was to get on the phone and tell this good news to all of my unsaved friends and relatives. My second reaction was, "How come they don't *already* understand something so basic and simple?" My third reaction was, "Maybe I had better get some training!" My wife shared my enthusiasm but lovingly reminded me I had a family and business that occasionally needed some attention. Fortunately for me, she was very willing to do much more than her share to keep our active family and business going.

Career-wise, I had spent ten years each with two top-notch companies. My specialty had become training professional salesmen and I had twenty years of the very best sales-training experience that one could hope for. About three years prior to my conversion, I had started my own sales-consulting firm. The backbone of that organization was to put on workshops and seminars for small businesses needing help in sales.

Actually, all we were doing was encouraging and motivating professional salesmen to do what they already knew how to do. The business was doing well and we had capable help, which gave me some freedom to pursue other interests.

One of the first things I did was to make arrangements to attend a week-long Lay Institute at Campus Crusade Headquarters at Arrowhead Springs in San Bernardino, California.

I had already been exposed to some of their excellent training materials and was impressed with the brochure describing the training so I had high expectations. As the program unfolded, I was not disappointed.

My business connections allowed me to be exposed

to some of the very best training seminars in the country. I could recognize a good training program and Campus Crusade's was excellent. A whole series of transferable concepts had been developed and fine-tuned so that anyone could teach them to others. The on-the-job training materials and techniques were as good as any I had seen in the secular world.

After a very thorough orientation, we were encouraged to practice what we had been taught. We were asked to go out in teams of two to verbalize The Four Spiritual Laws booklet with the folks in a particular section of town. As might be suspected, most of us panicked at the thought. I hasten to add that no one was forced to participate—strongly encouraged, but not coerced. My partner that day was a middle-aged pastor from a church of about three hundred people. With some reluctance, we convinced each other to do what we had been asked to do.

We were amazed at the receptivity of the people we visited. Most received us graciously. Several let us go through the entire booklet. The few who were negative assured us they were not offended by our visit. Most thanked us for our willingness to take the time to stop by. When we returned, we were again surprised to learn that every other team had mostly positive experiences as well.

My experience in training others made me very partial to any simple tool, but I must confess, I had some reservations about reading such a long booklet aloud, word for word. No doubt I was super-sensitive about the listener's attention span and concerned about criticism of a "canned pitch." Still I saw the wisdom of doing exactly what was suggested and, more importantly, I had seen some very positive results with my own eyes. Common sense dictated that I postpone any judgment of what was obviously an effective method and excellent evangelism tool.

I learned something else that day that has since been reconfirmed hundreds of times. The primary problem of visiting in the neighborhood is the *reluctance of church people,* not the receptivity of those in the community. It is true that some members of the community are understandably turned off by the pressure from some persistent organizations, but, for the most part, people in the neighborhood of a local church are flattered by a visit from friendly people from that church, particularly if they are not selling tickets or asking for money.

During that exciting week, a whole new avenue of interest was opened to me. I was already in the business of motivating people but was now beginning to realize the incredible potential for motivating church people to communicate the good news in a local neighborhood. Thanks to Campus Crusade for Christ, I was rather quickly made aware of the startling need for believers who were willing to work in the area of evangelism. I went away with my heart and head spinning.

Coming Face to Face With the Problem

During the next few months I read everything I could get my hands on that had anything to do with evangelism. "Evangelism Explosion" was in its infancy at that time but sounded interesting. I made arrangements to attend "A Celebration of Evangelism" in the midwest where Dr. D. James Kennedy was the featured speaker. I was impressed with Dr. Kennedy and very intrigued by his somewhat different, straightforward approach to presenting the gospel. Rather than waiting to attend a regional training session, which I did at a later date, I bought the training manual and went over it meticulously. I memorized all the required material and taught myself how to do the complete presentation exactly as recommended.

The next two years became a time of many changes for our family. During that first year we made a decision that took much prayer and caused a twinge of hurt in our parents. We left the denomination that had been a tradition on both sides of our family heritage. We joined a large, active, Bible-centered evangelical church. Looking back, we now realize that this church was almost a half-way house for our family. We were used to a very formal, almost rigid worship service. The church provided enough of what we considered to be "traditional" and blended it with strong biblical teaching and preaching.

As a direct result of a Christ-centered youth group there, our other two children also made a commitment to Christ. Now everyone in our family was actively involved in a fellowship and Bible study group.

I was asked to join the evangelism committee at the church. It was composed of fourteen very capable and loving men and women. I did not know it, and did not understand the significance of it at the time, but all of them were 10 percenters. As I was folded into this beautiful group of concerned Christians, they eventually shared some of their frustrations.

The twenty-four member church board was generous with funds for evangelism programs, but, with one exception, each member refused to become personally involved in any kind of evangelism training. The one exception was the chairman of our committee. As I pressed for a reason, the answers seemed to be that each board member was just too busy with another area of ministry or they would say, "Evangelism is just not my thing." I made up my mind to do some investigating on my own and made a fascinating discovery: The board members had done a super job of convincing each other they did not have to be personally involved in aggressive evangelistic outreach. In my thinking, it was strange that the leaders of a right-on evangelical church could have this attitude. Much to my sorrow, I discovered that this was not at all uncommon and that it transcended all denominations. It amazed me then, and still does today, that many evangelical leaders are convinced that the only ones who should personally lead others to Christ are those who have the gift of evangelism.

The leader's excuse is frequently, "I witness by my life. I'll tell them about my Christian experience or talk about my church when asked, but I don't feel called or qualified to do aggressive evangelism like so-and-so." This is frequently followed by the questionable statement, "Now, don't get me wrong. I'm in favor of evangelism training at our church. It should have high priority." What each leader was really saying was that everything possible should be done to get people trained to lead non-Christians to Christ, *As long as it isn't me!"*

The time came for me to take a trip back east. I had not been back to my home town since I had made my commitment. Fortunately I had been well indoctrinated that all evangelism must be steeped in prayer and done in the power of the Holy Spirit. So, I asked my family and many others to pray that the Holy Spirit would use me. Armed with a few good tracts, some excellent questions about eternal life, several memorized Scripture verses and my trusty Bible, I was determined to share the good news with some of my family and old friends. Oh, how I wish I had been able to have a concealed tape recorder.

Some of those early conversations were priceless. One of my first encounters was with my brother-in-law. I started to go over the "Four Spiritual Laws" booklet and was shocked when he told me he didn't believe in the resurrection. He was not happy when I informed him that he could not claim to be a Christian if he did not believe that Christ rose from the grave. He immediately accused me of being judgmental. I'm sorry to say the conversation went from bad to worse. Can't you just hear me? "The Bible says this! The Bible says that!" He told me he didn't care what the Bible said and concluded that I had become a religious fanatic . . . that sounded familiar.

My next encounter was with an old pal. Bob had been my closest friend for ten years prior to our move to California. We had a good reunion, talking about old times. My wife had written his wife about our experience of changing churches, so he eventually asked me about that. I tried to explain tactfully what had happened to our daughters and how we had attended the couples' conference. He listened attentively about our conversion experience. The timing seemed right so I plugged into some of my training and said, "Bob, have you come to a place in your spiritual life where you know for certain that if you were to die tonight you'd go to heaven?" He paused, looked me straight in the eye and said, "It's none of your blankety-blank business!" My instruction manual didn't tell me how to respond to that. He half-jokingly and half-seriously accused me of becoming another religious "kook" from California.

While this meeting didn't ruin our friendship, from that point on our joyful reunion became a strained conversation.

I'm happy to say I did have several positive experiences on that trip and even led one person to Christ. When I got back with the evangelism committee, I asked them to help me figure out what I had done wrong. The general consensus: nothing. I had just suffered for Jesus!

No doubt a little suffering can be experienced from time to time, but I knew there had to be a better way. I was determined to find out what I had done wrong and, more specifically, how I could share the truth of the gospel without getting people so upset. It took hundreds of gospel presentations and about five more years for me to find out.

Before the year was out, the church board did take some action in the area of evangelistic outreach. True to form, it required no personal involvement other than a yes vote. They hired Chuck, a gifted lay evangelist, to be the full-time minister of evangelism. He immediately went out and did a super job.

Every lead from the church was given to him and, within months, he personally led scores of people to Christ. I know of no one who does a more thorough job of leading people to the saving knowledge of Jesus Christ than this dedicated man. There was a standing invitation that he would take any interested Christian with him on his calls. I went with him frequently and loved to analyze his every move. He had an infinite number of ways to change the subject to spiritual things and joyfully admitted that he never presented the gospel the same way twice. Chuck is the personification of a perfect 10 percenter. For this reason, although he was a great inspiration to other Christians, it was impossible to duplicate his presentation. After going with him, most would say, "That was great. God certainly uses you in a marvelous way but *I could never do that.*" People like Chuck are mightily used of God but do not necessarily make good trainers.

Change of Plans

Another significant event was about to take place in my life. Bill, the chairman of the evangelism committee, had become my closest spiritual advisor. We frequently got together to talk so it did not surprise me when he suggested we have our periodic lunch date. During lunch, we discussed how a call to the ministry comes about and what it usually entails. He told me that it had become apparent to everyone on our committee that perhaps I was being called to a full- or part-time ministry of evangelism. In a way, I was surprised; in another way, I was not because my wife

and I had discussed that very same possibility. I told Bill that it seemed as if I were being challenged to discover the real reason for the evangelism blockage that was becoming so evident to me. I also told him of my conviction that the problem of individual apathy must first be dealt with at the local church level and that every member should be equipped by the church to do some form of one-on-one evangelistic outreach. Bill assured me this was 100 percent biblical.

You have to remember, of course, that at this time we had only partially identified the problem. The goal was clear—the solution still fuzzy.

We agreed that I should set up a small para-church organization separate from but under the wing of our church. I was pleasantly surprised to learn that Bill had already talked to the pastor about this possibility, and he had given his enthusiastic approval to the idea.

Incidentally, the reason for the recommendation for a para-church organization was not to get outside the jurisdiction of the church. Quite the contrary. We wanted to be able to work with churches across denominational lines and not identify with just one particular group.

Things seemed to be coming together nicely, but it was frightening to think of myself as a part-time minister.

Bill's counsel was to pray and let the Lord work out the details. The next week was most exciting. My wife and I prayerfully decided to put the entire consulting business up for sale. I knew too well that this would probably amount to nothing. The lion's share of any consulting business is the good will and reputation that has been personally developed; the prospects of finding a buyer were poor.

In spite of this, we told all of our clients and constituents that the business was available. We didn't even advertise it. I suppose it was like setting out a fleece because I can remember saying, "Okay, Lord, if you want me to get into your work full-time, go ahead and sell it, and we'll use the money to start a new ministry."

Two days later a young man walked into the office and said he was interested. I took out a piece of paper and wrote a realistic price on it. I said, "This is the price and I won't sell for one penny less. If you're still interested, I'll tell you everything you need to know."

Four days later he presented me with a check for the full amount. Praise God from whom all blessings flow! I found myself in full-time ministry before I knew what hit me. In 1970 my wife and I were miraculously converted. One year later, our business was miraculously converted.

I went from motivating business people to sell to motivating church people to harvest.

1. *Good News for Modern Man* (New York: American Bible Society, 1966).
2. The Four Spiritual Laws booklet (San Bernardino, CA: Campus Crusade for Christ, Inc., 1967).

T·H·R·E·E

"Man to Man"

*Go into all the world and preach
the gospel to all creation.*
—Mark 16:15

Almost immediately after selling my business I started working with eager men in my own church doing visitation in the surrounding neighborhood. We had numerous leads within a mile radius of the church building. We went visiting whenever we could form a team. We also found it effective and motivating to take teams of "experienced" men to other churches in our area. I'm using the word *experienced* with tongue in cheek. The main difference between these men and others is that they went out and overcame their initial fear and reluctance of sharing the gospel by simply doing it. I was personally surprised to see how easy it was to build a group of dedicated men who were willing to join a larger team that went from church to church.

Having chosen to start working almost exclusively with men, it seemed appropriate to call the ministry "Man to Man." The format was simple. Each participating church held a Saturday morning breakfast for twenty-four men. The church recruited twelve men; we brought in twelve men. During breakfast there was fellowship. After break-

37

fast, some of our men presented scriptural principles that showed the need to reach out. Next a short film, *Like a Mighty Army*,[1] dramatically illustrated a powerful conversion.

During the discussion that followed, it was agreed we all should be doing something similar to what we had just seen portrayed in the film. About 10:30 A.M. a representative from our group explained that we, the visiting group, would demonstrate how to talk to people in the neighborhood about Jesus Christ. In most cases, the men from the host church were not told ahead of time that they would be going out into the neighborhood. If they had been told, many would not have shown up. In each case, the pastor knew exactly what we intended to do and picked the neighborhood area he wanted us to cover. Usually we would go in a sunburst pattern around the church building.

After prayer, we went into the neighborhood in teams of two. We always had one experienced presenter teamed with one slightly bewildered observer. As we went to the doors of the homes closest to the church, we simply said that we were from Such-and-Such Church right down the street. They usually replied, "Oh sure, I know that church." We then asked permission to ask a few opinion questions. Some immediately said, "No thanks" and dismissed us.

The vast majority, however, agreed to talk with us. We then proceeded to ask some non-threatening opinion questions that had no right or wrong answers. We then asked permission to *briefly* share our answers to those same questions. By miraculous coincidence, the answers were summarized by the gospel. Upon returning to the church, the positive results always amazed us. Invariably the men from the church would say, "You know, that wasn't anywhere near as bad as I thought it was going to be."

Why was it that this experience was never anywhere near as threatening as most anticipated? After all, we were doing cold calling in a hostile jungle. When I told a group of midwestern pastors how we did this, they said "Well, California is different." That's very true. After living in California for twenty-five years, I can attest to that. But I've learned that the general reaction to simple *questions* about the gospel is the same no matter where you go in this country.

But as to why we were so well received, we still were not sure. We did not realize it at the time, but this was when we began to present the gospel in a non-threatening way. Everyone likes to give an opinion but many do not like to have their personal opinions challenged. We took advantage of this by first identifying ourselves as coming from a local, well-known, friendly church. This immediately took us out of the category of several other well-known door-to-door religious groups. We would then simply ask a few opinion questions, quickly adding that there are no right and wrong answers. (This technique allowed us to eliminate the occasional controversy concerning taking a survey.) Most people would immediately say, "Oh, that's good. What's the question?" Of course, some would say, "No, thank you," and we would politely take our leave by giving them a church brochure.

The questions we asked actually allowed us to get a fairly good idea of where people were spiritually, but that wasn't as important as the next question: "May we take a few more minutes to briefly tell you what we think *might* be good answers to those questions?" The key word here is *might*. We get away from making strong, dogmatic statements by simply suggesting that these answers *might* be better answers.

Asking permission to ask opinion questions and then again asking permission to give our opinion proved to be a very normal and natural way to sensitively approach people.

These "Man to Man" meetings were also the start of uncovering the 10 percent/90 percent concept. We were still not aware of it when it was happening, but it has since become obvious that *all* of our volunteers on those Saturday morning teams were 10 percenters.

With the pastor's permission, we would invite the men from each church to consider joining our traveling team. After most meetings, one person would come charging up to me and say, "That was great. It's about time we did something like that around here. I'd love to join the team. When is your next meeting?" You guessed it. He was a faithful 10 percenter. While we were at the church, the entire group was caught up in the enthusiasm. The pastors were greatly encouraged, but the desire to continue the program came from only a handful (10 percent).

Let's look at what happened. In each church we visited, usually one or two 10 percenters would truly get excited about what had been demonstrated. With the pastor's encouragement, these men would try to rally and motivate the group to continue what had been started. Predictably, their enthusiasm would be rapidly deflated by the blank stares of the 90 percenters who had attended the meeting but had no desire to do anything more. We now know we were experiencing the results of a basic premise: *You cannot force 90 percenters to do what 10 percenters love to do. It doesn't work and it never will.*

Even so, what we were doing still had an unusual appeal. But the effect of those Saturday morning "Man to Man" meetings was similar to what occurs when a guest evangelist is brought in to speak. Much excitement and enthusiasm are generated, but little or nothing is done after the evangelist is gone.

You would think that out of the more than one hundred churches we visited, at least *one* would be motivated enough to take the tools we had left and continue doing what we had demonstrated. Unfortunately, not one church was able to generate enough enthusiasm to ever give it a serious try.

In spite of the disappointments, many positive things occurred. In addition to the impact on the non-Christians, all those involved enjoyed special Christian fellowship and many positive evangelism experiences. It also provided great opportunities to develop and fine-tune the techniques that were to be used later in the harvesting ministry.

At the same time, though, I was getting more and more frustrated that so few believers were interested in evangelistic outreach.

1. *Like a Mighty Army* (Gospel Films, 1970).

F · O · U · R

Learning to
Labor Together

A house divided against itself falls.
— Luke 11:17

Stan and I had come to know each other well and had excellent rapport. As a fellow elder, Stan listened to my complaint about the lack of one-on-one evangelism at our church and understood my frustration with the leaders who refused to participate in any evangelism training.

Stan was also the person who made me aware of the real plight of the genuine 90 percenters.

By this time, we on the evangelism committee had started the "Evangelism Explosion" training in our church. We found it impossible to recruit any of the elders, including Stan. In the meantime, "Man to Man" meetings had caught on well. Several from our church were active as team members. Stan had talked to these men and was enthused enough to ask me if he could come to a Saturday morning breakfast meeting.

Stan was my partner and as we left the church he let me know in no uncertain terms that he liked everything he had seen so far but didn't like this door-to-door idea at all. On the way to the first house, I assured him that the people would probably be much more receptive than he expected. We said a quick prayer and went up to the first door. I did everything exactly according to the prescribed plan. Anyone who has done this kind of visiting knows that anything can happen but it usually doesn't.

During the visit, everything went so well it almost looked like a setup. We were warmly received, invited inside and had a cup of coffee with the man of the house. His wife was out shopping and the children were playing in the backyard. Casually we went through the procedure exactly according to the book. In a most matter-of-fact way, this gracious gentleman voluntarily answered all of our questions. When we came to the question about sin, he just said candidly that at this time in his life, he did not want to turn from sin.

We stopped and asked permission to send him information that would help him convince himself he should turn from sin. He agreed to that and we changed the subject. With a promise to send the information and a firm handshake, we thanked him and took our leave.

As we walked down the street, Stan said, "I can't believe it. That was *too* easy!" I had to admit that if I had written the script, I could not have come up with a more ideal demonstration.

Was that a typical visit? Absolutely not. There is no such thing. Everyone is unique. This was, however, quite similar to many of the visits we had made over a year's time.

It was a positive experience because we were able to articulate the gospel and in the process find out exactly where this pre-Christian was in relationship to Jesus Christ. We were able to do this in a way that was completely non-confrontive and we accomplished it in a matter of minutes, not hours or months. This call was ideal because as soon as we reached our objective, we stopped. This eliminated any kind of confrontation. Because a non-threatening dialogue was used, it was inappropriate to try to nail the person or win points of argument.

A confronter (10 percenter) may well have been frustrated by this approach, which apparently had inconclusive results. He may have taken the opportunity to convince the same individual of the need to recognize sin and immediately repent. This, of course, is thoroughly biblical and, at times, desirable.

However, the non-confronter as well fulfills God's commission by carefully discovering where the individual is in relationship to Jesus Christ. As the Holy Spirit prepares the harvest, there are various stages through which a pre-Christian progresses. Once we discover where the person is stopped in this process, we ask permission to provide information in the form of the printed page to help remove the blockage and then change the subject. In some cases, the pre-Christian is ready to receive Christ. In other cases, he may not have progressed sufficiently and needs encouragement, not confrontation.

At the next two houses on our visitation, no one was home. An older woman at the fourth house said, "How nice of you to come. I appreciate the thought but I'm not interested right now. Maybe some other time."

Time was running out so we started back. "I really can't believe it," Stan said once more. "I never had any idea it could be so easy. Nobody got mad at us."

Back at the church during the brief sharing time, one of the men bubbled as he told about a man and his wife who had just made a commitment to Jesus Christ. "And they meant it!" exclaimed his partner. One team had a door slammed in their face, but most of the other reports were more positive than negative.

A few days later, Stan and I had lunch. Guess what he said about the door-to-door visiting? "I couldn't believe how easy it was." Then he said something very interesting. Even though our visit was a positive experience and even though he was enthusiastic, he could not and would not want to do it again. He would never volunteer.

I said, "If you can tell me why you feel so strongly about this, it would be very helpful."

He thought for a few minutes and said, "I'm not sure I can put my finger on it. It's just something I definitely would not choose to do. I don't think it's because I'm scared," he went on to say. "I admire you and the others, but it's just not for me." Then he added something that may have been prophetic: *"I'm sure all of the other elders would feel exactly the same way."*

We talked about the drive and enthusiasm of the individual team members, who, of course, all were 10 percenters. I don't know what made me say it, but I asked, "How do you really feel about our team members? Are they a threat to you? Am I a threat to you?" His candid reply was, "Yes, in a way you are." He went on to explain again that he appreciated every one of us, but perhaps we should try not to push others into doing things that we like to do if it made the others feel uncomfortable.

The loving intent of this conversation was confirmed over and over again by other 90 percenters and allowed me to discover three very important pieces of the puzzle:

- Ninety percenters feel uncomfortable doing door-to-door-work; therefore, they should be taken only on visits where they are expected.

- Ninety percenters feel uncomfortable talking to strangers; therefore, they should be encouraged to work with people they know already.

- Ninety percenters appreciate 10 percenters but actually feel threatened by them; therefore, when it comes to evangelism training, we should always let 10 percenters equip 10 percenters and 90 percenters equip 90 percenters.

The 10 Percent Personality

Later in the ministry, two men, Bill and Terry, and their pastor helped me appreciate how most 10 percenters feel in the same way Stan helped me understand how 90 percenters feel.

Bill had been a very active team member in the early days until the national company he worked for transferred him to Pennsylvania. After being there a few years, he was made chairman of his church board. By phone, I told him of some of the changes since those Saturday morning "Man to Man" meetings. He liked the idea of a non-confrontive evangelism seminar and convinced the pastor and Terry, the chairman of the evangelism committee, to let me come and present it.

The 10 percent/90 percent idea was new to Bill, but he was open to it and was sure that equipping 90 percenters would be a good idea.

I arrived a day before the seminar was scheduled. This allowed for a joyful reunion and a meeting with Bill and his pastor. Unfortunately, Terry was out of town. As I explained our emphasis on using a non-confrontive plan, a problem started to surface. Terry was, without a doubt, an unusually strong 10 percenter. They described how he had strong motivation and definite plans to teach everyone in the church to become a "soul winner." Both of them knew that Terry had a tremendous love for the Lord and the lost and that he was in favor of *anything* that brings people to Christ.

Without even meeting Terry, I could see how perfectly he fit our extra-aggressive, 10 percent mold. Based on past experiences with others like him, I knew it would be necessary to carefully fill him in on exactly what we were trying to accomplish. When an aggressive 10 percenter is in charge of evangelism, it is absolutely essential to prepare him ahead of time. We can assume that as the non-confrontive plan unfolds during the seminar, he will not like it. If we didn't convince him that at least some of his people needed the non-confrontive plan, he would be apt to stand right up in the middle of the meeting and say the church doesn't want this kind of training.

Bill and the pastor agreed that Terry should be filled in about this particular evangelism approach because he would normally speak his mind. The problem was that Terry was scheduled to arrive just before the meeting and even expected to be a little late. I went on to explain how the 90 percenters would love a non-confrontive approach, but the reaction of a genuine 10 percenter is predictable. They may not like the simplified plan of salvation because it tends to box them in. They would also actually resent the suggestion to back off when the non-Christian has an objection.

I suggested that we use Terry as a test case. They both agreed that it might be fun and assured me that Terry was strong and understanding enough to be our guinea pig. However, as a precaution, Bill asked Terry not to make any comments during my presentation.

Terry arrived just before the seminar started and greeted me warmly. I made a point of not staring at him during the presentation, but sure enough, as the meeting progressed, I could sense his uneasiness.

When the seminar was over, Bill and the pastor stood near me. Almost as if it were written in a script, several 90 percenters came up and said, "This is great. This is exactly what we need. How come we haven't heard something like this before?"

Terry slowly worked his way toward us. When he got to me I said, "Terry, please be very truthful. I need to have your honest, candid opinion on two questions. How do you like this simple harvesting tool?"

He said, "Well, frankly, I don't."

I said, "Okay, now please tell me how you feel about backing off when there's an objection."

Without a bit of hesitation, he replied, "I don't like that either. I could never do it!"

The three of us burst out laughing. The pastor quickly explained our little game. They were right. Terry was not offended and the four of us will never forget the good lesson learned. The 10 percenter's reaction is completely appropriate once it is understood.

I received a letter from Bill several weeks later, which said in part: "Terry is still in cement over the simplicity of the concept, but he has agreed to let me handle the training of the 90 percenters. Our primary objective is to train people who can train others. 2 Timothy 2:2."

For some, like Terry, soul winning is a major goal. Ten percenters lovingly confront people with the reality of the gospel on a regular basis and make a concerted effort to talk about salvation. On the opposite end of the scale are the 90 percenters who, just like Stan, believe that their lives and friendly attitudes do it all.

Back to the Basics

Another very positive thing happened as a result of "Man to Man" experiences. Both before and after most of those meetings, I had a rare opportunity to spend quality time with the pastors. In the quiet of their offices or in the relaxed atmosphere of a restaurant, we talked about the frustration that surrounds evangelism.

These private discussions with the pastors and open discussions with the laymen centered around what's wrong with this, what's wrong with that, I like this, I don't like that. Most of us are open and willing to listen to new ideas, but have you noticed? When it comes to evangelism, we are usually very set in our ways.

I'm not complaining about this, mind you, but I spent three years actually *soliciting* grass roots complaints about evangelism at the local church. I think it's safe to say that I heard every conceivable complaint and excuse that has ever been made about almost every evangelism method or tool. As a result, I began to see some things that could and *should* be changed.

Still, these things seemed to be mostly surface problems. It was becoming apparent that a hyped-up, one-shot program would not do the job. My desire was to get to the root of the problem, but it became more and more evident that the root system was complex.

It was like a giant picture puzzle. Some areas were not completed. Were some of the pieces missing or just too difficult to locate?

I became obsessed with finding the elusive pieces to complete that puzzle. I confess I was becoming disturbed that it wasn't coming together faster. To expedite the process, I started reading everything I could get my hands on that had anything to do with evangelism. I had already read much but with the help of my pastor friends and several seminary libraries, I discovered mountains of information that few church people ever see. The more I read, the more frustrated I became.

Each writer seemed to make the job more and more

complex, while my desire was to make everything as simple and uncomplicated as possible. When I applied the 10 percent/90 percent idea to the most weighty theological evangelism enigmas, it changed the whole perspective. Almost everything I read could have been dramatically revolutionized if the 10 percent/90 percent concept had been utilized.

I also had a personal wrestling match with the many questions created by 1 Corinthians 2:14:

> But a natural man does not accept the things of the Spirit of God; for they are foolishness to him, and he cannot understand them, because they are spiritually appraised.

It took several months for me to come to a conclusion that was personally satisfactory. It is a weighty theological subject, but the bottom line is that the simple gospel message is not foolishness to some pre-Christians. Everything else is.

I could see no reason why it is necessary to have literally hundreds of different gospel presentations, with almost as many different ways to approach people. It seemed to me that a biblical plan of salvation could be standardized and still be impeccable. At the same time, we discovered other simple concepts that were guaranteed to keep Christians from getting bogged down in arguments and worthless discussions.

More importantly, I now realize that the complaints I had been hearing over the years were the key to solving the puzzle. If I could objectively evaluate these complaints, if I could just determine which ones were truly legitimate, perhaps the puzzle could be solved.

F • I • V • E

Harvesting: Non-Confrontive Evangelism

Behold, I say to you, lift up your eyes, and look on the fields, that they are white for harvest.
—John 4:35

Reflecting back on those Saturday morning "Man to Man" meetings, I realize how important they were to the harvesting breakthrough.

After a hearty breakfast and lively conversation around the table, it was natural to start our formal program with an open discussion. We would ask the group to share their evangelism experiences.

At one particular meeting there was no response from the group we were visiting. The silence was deafening. Finally, a man in the back of the room could not contain himself any longer. He was a big, tough, lovable construction worker who tells it like it is!

"Why are there so many different ways to do evangelism?" he wanted to know. "Everyone I've ever talked

51

with seems to have a different idea about what's the best way, but I don't see them doing it. I'm on the Evangelism Committee here, and frankly, I'm confused and very discouraged."

I don't think I've ever heard it articulated more candidly than that, but his sentiments have been expressed over and over again. We were meeting with groups of very dedicated men. Their love of the Lord and their commitment were evident. But when it came to evangelism, most were confused and discouraged.

We on the "Man to Man" teams had a strong desire to turn this around. What better way than to go right back to the basics. What better way than to go right back to Scripture!

We used several key verses to encourage and motivate us: John 4:35 says that the fields are already white (or ripe) for harvest; Luke 10:2 says that the laborers are few; Matthew 28:19 and Mark 16:15 tell us to go do it; 2 Timothy 2:2 tells us to equip each other to do all these things.

We were confident that our "Man to Man" approach was very biblical. We got excited about the fact that God has already prepared His harvest field. All He is asking us to do (actually *commanding* us to do) is to go out and pick the ripe fruit in His field.

As we went into the neighborhoods surrounding each church, we were simply checking the fruit. If it was ripe, we picked it. If not, we asked permission to do something that would help ripen it and then would leave it alone. Most of us had already learned how easy it is to bruise unripe fruit.

Due to the experiences we had, we developed this definition of harvesting:

Harvesting

Locating those whom God has prepared and prayerfully bringing them to commitment to Jesus Christ in the power of the Holy Spirit, according to scriptural recommendations, and encouraging those who are not yet ready.

The more we worked with this harvesting idea, the more we liked it. It slowly occurred to me that harvesting, as we had come to understand it, was different from other types of outreach. We were not doing aggressive *soul winning,* and we were not just *witnessing;* we were *harvesting.*

Let's take a closer look at the terms *soul winning* and *witnessing.* Even though it does frighten the average 90 percenter, soul winning is biblical. Proverbs 11:30 says: "He who is wise wins souls." *Soul winning* is a rather aggressive term and adequately describes what our eager 10 percenters enjoy doing.

Witnessing is not something we purpose to do — we're doing it all the time. We *are* witnesses. At times, we're good witnesses (or examples) and at other times we may not be so good. In any event, we have no choice as to whether we're a witness or not. We are witnessing whenever we are in contact with others.

Most evangelical church members and many leaders have convinced themselves that they are doing what God wants them to do by just being a good witness. The feeling that one is a good witness may bring satisfaction, but it is not what the Lord has commanded us to do. Jesus expresses His concern about our complacency. After assuring us that He has prepared the harvest, He points out that too few of us are willing to bring in the harvest He has prepared.

Jesus Christ expects us to be more than just a witness; in fact, He commands us to be active workers in His harvest field:

- Do you not say, "There are yet four months, and then comes the harvest"? Behold, I say to you, lift up your eyes and look on the fields, that they are white for harvest (John 4:35).
- The harvest is plentiful, but the workers are few (Matthew 9:37).
- I sent you to reap that for which you have not labored (John 4:38).
- Go into all the world and preach the Gospel to all creation (Mark 16:15).

The Birth of the Harvesting Seminar

Some years back, I had the opportunity to fly free to Guatemala. Our church supported several missionary organizations there, and I knew someone who might help me plan an itinerary. David Jones, an area director for InterVarsity, had spent several years in Central America. I had known Dave for some time and we had a successful "Man To Man" meeting at his church, so I didn't hesitate to ask for his help. He was thrilled to know I was going and immediately made all the arrangements. I would stay with a missionary, visit a Christian school and radio station, have a tour of an area that had been damaged by a major earthquake and then visit one of the tribes.

There was, however, one catch. He had phoned a friend at the seminary in Guatemala City. It just so happened that there was a conference at the seminary that ended the day I was to arrive. Twelve area directors from Central America Mission would be there. They were coming to develop programs to assist the pastors in their areas to do evangelism and discipleship. Dave had already volunteered my services.

He told his friend I would put on a Harvesting Seminar for these men on Friday night. I told Dave I couldn't speak a word of Spanish and that I didn't have a "Harvesting Seminar."

"No problem. They all understand English," said Dave. "Just tell them all the good things you told us about harvesting when you were at my church. That's exactly what they need to hear."

He went on to tell me that I would probably come unglued when I saw firsthand how ripe the fruit is in Central America. The non-Christians there are much more receptive and open to the gospel message than the ones in our country. Not only that, but these men were so pleased that I was coming to talk about harvesting that they all agreed to stay an extra night to hear me.

I panicked and got busy writing a seminar. The material that had been developed for our Saturday morning meetings was rather basic and was presented in a very casual way. My presentation in Guatemala would have to be different—something more detailed. My wife helped me with some notes, a simple agenda and an outline that I could hand out to everyone present. I packed my bag and before I knew it, I was in Guatemala City.

Talk about the V.I.P. treatment! I was met at the airport by a delightful young missionary couple and was ushered to their small but immaculate apartment. I would be their guest. "Our six-year-old loves to give up his bed for those funny people from the States," they exclaimed. After dinner, I was whisked to the seminary and sure enough, twelve bright-eyed young men were assembled at the conference table waiting to hear "the great harvester" from California, U.S.A. Let's face it—I was very nervous. I had forgotten how gracious these people are. I had been in Panama briefly during the war, so it should not have surprised me that they would put me completely at ease. They were exceedingly attentive as I presented my material.

As the evening concluded, they thanked me profusely. The leader of the group said, "What you don't know is that we've been praying for years that God would show us a way to more effectively harvest. This is exactly what you've done. We believe God sent you to us in answer to our prayers." Now I did come unglued. My heart melted.

On Saturday I had a complete sight-seeing tour of the old and new city. Early Sunday morning we went up the mountain to a tribal village. At the native church, I had the privilege of addressing the three hundred radiant Christians through a translator. Each person was dressed in brilliant native garb. I shall never forget the experience.

After the service, I was introduced to a one-hundred-year-old man who was one of the first from the tribe to be converted through the efforts of Wycliffe Translators.

When I got on the return flight on Monday I was a changed man and had a changed ministry.

Asking the Right Questions

Back in California, a special board meeting was called to hear a glowing report about the Guatemala "Harvesting Seminar." It was decided at that meeting to stop our Saturday morning meetings and expand the Harvesting Seminar. Invitations were sent to one hundred pastors to attend a demonstration of the Harvesting Seminar to be held at Simpson College in San Francisco. Forty pastors came, which exceeded our wildest expectations. Happily, the response was very favorable, and we were off and running in a slightly new direction but with the exact same goal.

Non-confrontive harvesting was becoming our specialized ministry. The Harvesting Seminar allowed us to get closer to our goal. The puzzle was now coming together.

As the ministry began to focus more and more on the specifics of effective harvesting, we started looking at different ways to present the actual words of the gospel. I theorized that perhaps the key was to ask questions rather than make strong biblical statements.

I had no intention of using him as an experiment, but I had developed a deep concern for a close friend, Ted Lott. When we first moved to California, Ted and his wife, Sigrid, became our closest friends. Our children attended the same school so our families got together frequently.

One day Ted agreed to have lunch with me. He was an insurance agent and worked in San Francisco. Our luncheon date was at a typically busy downtown restaurant. Our time together started with the usual pleasantries until he said rather abruptly, "Well, Walter, are you going to try to convert me today?" I am not usually one who is at a loss for words but this slowed me down. I must confess I had every intention of trying to present the gospel that day, but his candor took me by surprise. My mind flashed back to some of the blunders I had made in the past. I thought of the fiasco with my close friend, Bob, on the east coast. I certainly didn't want a repeat of that performance.

I looked at Ted and said, "No, I'm not going to try to convert you, but I'd like to ask you some very direct questions about spiritual things. Would that be all right?" His reply was instrumental in eventually modifying my concept of harvesting. He said he would be glad to answer my questions *as long as I didn't criticize his answers.* Without giving it a lot of thought, I said, "Okay, I'll try to ask only opinion questions."

I took out a copy of the Steps to Peace With God booklet.[1] You may have seen this booklet with its excellent visual diagram of how Jesus Christ bridges the gap between God and man. Instead of taking the time to go over that portion, I turned immediately to the last few pages where it itemizes four things one must do in order to receive Jesus Christ. I simply converted them into candid, straightforward opinion questions.

"Do you admit you are a sinner?"

Ted answered, "Well, it depends on what you mean by sin."

I said, "Okay, it means anything I do that separates me from God. I do things that separate me from God; therefore, I'm a sinner. Are you a sinner?"

"Oh, yes. There's no doubt about it," he said.

"Okay," I replied. "Are you willing to turn from sin?" We discussed that briefly, and he agreed he would genuinely like to try to turn away from sin.

The third question was, "Do you believe that Jesus Christ died for you on the cross and rose from the grave?"

Ted answered, "Oh yes. I've always believed that."

The final question was, "Would you be willing to say this prayer inviting Jesus Christ to come in and control your life as Savior and Lord?"

At this point, I remembered how Howard Ball had cautioned me at the couples' retreat. I parroted him by saying, "Please don't say this prayer unless you really mean it." Ted took the booklet and read the prayer very carefully to himself. After a few thoughtful moments he said, "Sure, I can do that, but do I have to do it right now?"

"No, you don't," I assured him, "but if you can in good conscience say it right now aloud, I wish you would. I'll show you why it's important in just a minute."

In the hustle and bustle of that busy restaurant, Ted Lott bowed his head and said, "Dear Lord Jesus, I know I am a sinner and need Your forgiveness. I believe You died for my sins. I now invite You to come into my life. I want to trust You as Savior and follow You as Lord and live in the fellowship of Your church. Amen."

I then turned back one page and read, "If you confess with your mouth Jesus as Lord, and believe in your heart that God raised Him from the dead, you shall be saved" (Romans 10:9). I explained that this verse is the reason it was important for him to say that prayer out loud. We went on to read another important truth:

> He who has the Son has the life; he who does not have the Son of God does not have the life. These things I have written to you who believe in the name of the Son of God, in order that you may know that you have eternal life (1 John 5:12,13).

All I had done was ask Ted four simple questions, after getting his permission. He could not in good conscience say no to any one of them. Within the next few months, Ted's wife, Sigrid, made a similar commitment, as did his children. That was almost fifteen years ago. Not too long ago, Ted died of a massive brain tumor. As he lay in a hospital bed and slowly slipped into unconsciousness, his only concern was that everyone who came into that room knew Jesus Christ as Lord and Savior.

Questions Rather Than Statements

The experience of helping Ted make a sincere commitment to Christ enabled me to see that what we had been using in the past fell short of what we were now trying to accomplish. Although existing tools were excellent for soul winning and witnessing, they were insufficient for harvesting. The problem with these excellent materials was that they made *statements of fact* concerning salvation. Although these statements were all positive and true, they created problems for us.

We discovered that for a non-confrontive approach, our main procedure for communicating salvation information was not primarily by making statements. Instead, we were discovering how to ask *probing, non-threatening questions*. This allowed us to stay on target without getting into trouble. By gently asking the right questions, we could usually discover exactly where the non-Christian was spiritually without getting into a confrontive situation.

Again, one of the ways of accomplishing this was to assure the non-Christian that there are no right or wrong answers to our questions. We would never condemn or criticize anyone for giving us an honest answer. Instead, recognizing the diagnostic character of our questions, we could proceed to sensitively handle each individual case in a non-threatening manner.

This interaction with Ted helped me to see something else that had been bothering me. No doubt Ted, like myself, had been exposed to the gospel message many times and in many ways. Why did we both neglect something as great as salvation for half a lifetime? Why do we Christians not encourage our friends, neighbors and relatives, who may well be ready, to consider something as critical and urgent as the saving of their soul?

Back to the Basics, Again

The problem is that when Christians try to articulate these details, they frequently become confused about what is essential for someone else to make a biblical commitment to Christ. Even those who have a good handle on the biblical requirements are often thrown off track by an off-the-wall comment or question that confuses the issue.

This is why it is so urgent to lovingly articulate exactly what is necessary to receive Christ. It is equally important for the harvester to be very aware of what is *not* necessary and how to avoid needless discussions which cause confusion.

To be effective in the harvest field, Christians must stay with the basics and minimize any confusion that might keep those whom the Holy Spirit has prepared from receiving Christ. Bill Bright writes about the power of simplicity in *Witnessing Without Fear:*

> As Vonette and I launched the ministry of Campus Crusade for Christ at UCLA in 1951, we learned very quickly that college students . . . weren't impressed with a complex, philosophical communication of the gospel.
>
> What impressed them was Jesus Christ—who He is, what He did for them, and how they can know Him.[2]

Developing the Harvesting Tool

A pastor in Concord, California, was very enthusiastic about our work from the start. Bob Parma had a passion for reaching the folks in the neighborhood of his church. He encouraged me to use the harvesting techniques for community visitation. We had learned that going in teams of three, two women and one man or two men and one woman, was most effective. Whenever we could arrange it, we would go with the people of his church.

One day, as Pastor Parma and I mused over an endless cup of coffee, we decided to try to come up with the perfect harvesting tool, starting a project that was to take several months. We theorized we needed to list the things that are absolutely necessary for someone to receive Christ and our challenge to one another was to itemize only the things that are biblically essential. We wanted to be able to say that in order to receive Jesus Christ, one need not do any *more* than this and one cannot do any *less* than this.

At the time, Pastor Parma was right in the middle of working on his doctorate. He had already decided to use harvesting as a part of his thesis, so he was in favor of researching anything that would help clarify the subject. We reminded ourselves that we did not want merely to change around words, phrases and Scripture verses. Thousands of tracts have been written and rewritten to come up with the perfectly worded plan of salvation.

Although what we were attempting seemed simple enough, we were dealing with some of the heaviest theological issues of all time: the atonement, blood sacrifice, propitiation, repentance, justification by faith, etc. We felt it was unnecessary to offer a theological explanation to a non-Christian as to how or why these things came about. Instead, we were trying to ascertain all the things and *only those things* absolutely essential for a life-saving commitment to Jesus Christ.

The project started to get touchy because we were reducing everything to its simplest common denominator. It was our desire to make this as basic as possible, and that meant leaving out some favorite verses. It also left us open to the criticism that we might be diluting the gospel.

We solicited the help of another close friend, Pastor Jim Cecy. When Pastor Cecy got involved, he put his creative genius to work and came up with the acrostic BAAAA. The arrangement of the first letters and verses proved to be the key to our harvesting tool, as we'll see in the next chapter.

---

1. Steps to Peace With God booklet (Minneapolis: Billy Graham Evangelistic Association). For more information on this booklet, write to the Billy Graham Evangelistic Association, Box 779, Minneapolis, Minnesota 55440.
2. Bill Bright, *Witnessing Without Fear* (San Bernardino, CA: Here's Life Publishers, 1987), p. 105.

S·I·X

BAAAA

Now is the day of salvation.
— 2 Corinthians 6:2

Five simple words and five biblical mandates summarize God's perfect harvesting plan:

- **B**elieve that Jesus Christ died on the cross, was buried and rose from the grave (1 Corinthians 15:3,4).
- **A**dmit sin (Romans 3:23).
- **A**gree to turn from sin to God through faith in Jesus Christ (Acts 20:21).
- **A**cknowledge Jesus Christ as Lord and Savior (Romans 10:9).
- **A**ccept the free gift of salvation (Ephesians 2:8,9).

The development of BAAAA turned out to be a major breakthrough. It was the pivotal point in creating a simple tool to equip 90 percenters to harvest, and it allowed us to make significant changes in our training techniques.

The Difference

Many salvation plans immediately hit the non-

Christian smack in the face with the sin issue. Before the sting has gone away, an even more threatening repentance demand is made. Acknowledging sin and being willing to turn from it are essential to salvation; however, Pastor Cecy encouraged us to put the "believe" issue first, which allows the plan to unfold with less of a threat.

Through BAAAA, we have a way to sensitively determine if the fruit in the harvest field is green, ripe or rotten. What makes the harvesting plan unique is that salvation verses are carefully presented in a way that is comfortable for the 90 percenter. As the BAAAA statements are converted into diagnostic questions, an honest response provides an efficient way to determine where the individual is in relationship to Jesus Christ without getting into controversy. Because there are no right or wrong answers, the questions, when asked in a non-confrontive way, are non-threatening.

The letters used and even the Scriptures that the words introduce are not some magic formula. I am often asked if I use other gospel presentations. Most certainly! The Four Spiritual Laws and Steps to Peace With God booklets are my favorites, and I use them often. I've found, though, that for effective non-confrontive harvesting, BAAAA works best. It is a tool which determines readiness and allows pre-Christians to receive Christ—two key points in this type of evangelism.

No Time Like the Present

One experience typifies how easy it is to convince ourselves that non-Christians might not be ready to receive Christ. I had occasion to work on a committee with a pastor friend. I showed him my material. He said, "Your literature looks great on the surface, but I feel you have the same problem as many other groups. Basically, you're encouraging 'easy believism.' "

I suggested we have a relaxing lunch together to discuss this possibility. During lunch, he told me that in seminary he had written a major paper on building bridges for friendship evangelism. His emphasis was on discovering creative ways to slowly and methodically lead non-Christians on a step-by-step journey until they were ready to be folded into the flock. As our discussion continued, there was no real conflict, but we lovingly wrestled with two extremes.

His platform was that for a solid commitment to be properly established, it usually takes effort and time. My platform was, "I agree in principal, but what about all those who have been ripe for some time, and we do everything else *except* pick the fruit?"

"Well, of course," he admitted, "occasionally some will be ripe, but let me give you an example of what I mean." That morning he had had breakfast with a non-Christian businessman for the second time. He told me a little about this man's complicated background and said, "I feel confident this guy will soon come to Christ. He's letting me help him work through the many questions he has about spiritual things; that takes time. He just isn't ready."

I paused, smiled and said, "Pastor, may I have your permission to back you right into a corner?"

He laughed and said, "Sure. You've done it at our committee meetings without asking permission! Go ahead."

"Did you ask him if he believes that Christ died on the cross for him and rose from the grave?"

"Oh yes. He definitely does," he replied.

"Did you ask him if he's a sinner?"

"Definitely. He's admitted that several times."

"Did you ask him if he's willing to turn from sin?"

"No, I have never asked him that."

In a loving way I said, "Then, you cannot know that he is not ready to make a commitment to Jesus Christ."

He put his hands up in the air and said, "You got me!"

Now, of course, the man may not have been ready to turn from sin that particular day. Neither of us knew for sure. The point is *we really don't know until we ask.*

This good friend of mine immediately realized the only reason I challenged him and made this bold accusation was not to embarrass him but to edify us both. We sat there in amazement and thanked God for a simple illustration of how easy it is to miss picking the ripe fruit. Sometimes the ripe fruit is easy to overlook.

The need to always be ready to take immediate action was brought home to me when my wife had an extended stay in the hospital. The woman across the hall had terminal cancer and often returned my cheery hellos and waves as I passed back and forth. My wife and I agreed that I should talk to her. As my wife prayed, I stepped in and asked permission to ask her some questions about spiritual things. She responded positively to BAAAA and made a sincere commitment.

The next day her husband arrived and beckoned me into the hall. He was furious. His wife had tried to tell him that she now knew Jesus, but he wanted no part of it. He pointed his finger at me and said sternly, "You keep your religion to yourself, mister. Don't go bothering my wife about religion. She's got enough to worry about." Three days later she died. If she honestly and sincerely meant it when she said yes to those five questions, she has nothing to worry about now. I pray that someone will reach her husband with the same good news before it's too late.

S·E·V·E·N

A Transferable
Tool

*And the things which you have heard from me
in the presence of many witnesses,
these entrust to faithful men,
who will be able to teach others also.*
—2 Timothy 2:2

In an earlier chapter, we stressed that the answers to opinion questions are not right or wrong. This is a true statement, provided the questions are worded properly. Generally speaking, people love to give their opinion. There will usually be some reluctance, however, if the one being questioned feels that his opinion might be challenged.

This was brought home strongly for me while living in the New England states. The mindset of the traditional New England Yankee is, "I'll answer any question you ask me. Just don't make fun of my answers!" Getting permission and then sensitively asking questions is an excellent way to find out about someone. *Telling* someone something is sometimes an ineffective way of communicating life-changing information.

Making the Tool

An easy way to present BAAAA is on a 3x5 card. The 3x5 card (see *Figure 3* for text) is an effective hand-held visual that has been prayerfully designed to enable the harvester to stay right on track without being the least bit pushy. The card is held so both people can see it. Then the first question is asked, "Do you believe that Jesus Christ died on the cross for you and rose from the grave?" If the person says *yes*, the next question is asked, "Do you admit you are a sinner?" If he says *yes* again, the next question is asked, "Do you agree to turn from sin?" And so on.

If the pre-Christian says *no* to any one of these five questions, it is important not to overreact but to simply and calmly say, "I appreciate your honesty. If I could give you information that would help you convince yourself that (whatever the objection is), would you read it?" The subject is then promptly changed back to secular things and no comments are made about the negative reply.

God's Perfect Plan

Do you . . .

- **Believe** Jesus Christ died on the cross for you and rose from the grave? (Jesus "rose" physically from the grave after three days.) (1 Corinthians 15:3,4)

- **Admit** you are a sinner? (Do you do things God does not like?) (Romans 3:23)

- **Agree** to turn from sin to God? (Are you willing to turn away from things that God does not like, as best you know how, right now?) (Acts 20:21)

- **Acknowledge** Jesus is Lord? (Are you willing to turn your life over to God and let Him run it?) (Romans 10:9)

- **Accept** God's free gift of salvation? (It's a free gift—no strings attached. You cannot "earn" it.) (Ephesians 2:8,9)

Will you say this simple prayer aloud?

Lord Jesus, I receive you as my Lord and personal Savior. Amen.

Figure 3

When working with the BAAAA card, it is usually not necessary to amplify or elaborate. From time to time, a simple explanation may be required, but the 3x5 card basically doesn't need great elaboration (see Appendix C, *Figure E)*. Nor does the card require involved instructions for its use. It can be tucked into a wallet and referred to frequently. When read over and over again, it becomes a natural part of the harvesting experience.

It is comforting to know that the whole gospel message is at your finger tips. At any time, it can be presented in a matter of minutes and the fear that an important point may be forgotten is eliminated. The harvester is always ready to help someone come to Christ — whenever, wherever they may happen to be.

As we start asking the questions on this card, it is easy to see how its logical questions allow for a meaningful response without causing controversy.

Sensitivity Built Right In

In spite of this, some Christians still seem to be threatened by the "mechanics" of any plan. Perhaps they feel it is too impersonal or that someone might try to force them to do something that might make them feel uncomfortable. Even though these thoughts probably stem from past negative experiences, they are still very real to a person who is trying something he has never used before.

Let's take a look at what *really* happens in a harvesting experience. First of all, it is completely appropriate to politely ask permission to ask a question. It is highly improbable that anyone will be offended by that. At this point, we only ask questions that can be answered *yes* or *no* with no right or wrong answers. We are simply looking for honest answers to opinion questions. If at any time we receive a *no* answer, we immediately terminate the spiritual discussion.

The exciting thing about harvesting is that when asking the diagnostic questions, we frequently get yes answers because God has faithfully prepared His harvest. The BAAAA card provides questions to ask that allow us to know exactly what to do next. We can feel comfortable and confident because no matter what the non-Christian says, we know precisely how to respond. Because we only move ahead with permission and always back off when there is a negative response, the non-Christian doesn't have a reason to get upset with us, and the Christian has no reason to feel embarrassed.

This presentation protects harvesters from becoming insensitive. It literally keeps us from saying anything that is unnecessary, inappropriate, threatening or confrontational.

Harvesters do not move until a green light is given. When there is a red light, we must stop. For example, when a person says no to the direct BAAAA question, it means there is at least *one* reason he is not yet ready to receive Christ. Instead of overreacting to the no answer, we simply acknowledge it, casually offer to send specific information that will help him zero in on that particular need and stop. It is completely unnecessary, if not foolish, to give information that answers questions he is not asking.

A confronter, instead of offering to send information, has a strong desire to comment about the consequences of saying no. Instead of bringing in someone else in the form of a printed page, the confronter is able to quote a page or two from a book on apologetics. This is not to say that this is bad. It is, however, a *soul winner's* approach and quite different from *harvesting*.

What if someone just keeps saying *yes* to all of the BAAAA questions? What is done then? When this happens,

God is allowing us to see the Holy Spirit work in the heart of a pre-Christian. We now have the great joy and privilege of helping that person receive Jesus Christ and the free gift of eternal life. Is anything in heaven or earth more valuable or rewarding than this?

What I have been describing here is certainly not a mindless, mechanical exercise. Instead, it is a sensitive, systematic procedure that is truly non-threatening to the Christian and non-Christian alike.

This makes me think of an airplane. BAAAA is like a super-sensitive automatic pilot. The 3x5 card helps take us exactly where we are supposed to go but quickly and gently stops us if there is a problem ahead because the individual is not ready.

After a thorough explanation of the harvesting procedure, it is not uncommon for someone to say, "All that is fine, but I wait for the Holy Spirit to tell me what to say." It isn't wise to challenge a statement like this because the Holy Spirit does guide us. On the other hand, the Holy Spirit has already made it crystal clear that God wants all Christians to articulate the truth of God's perfect plan. We should be well prepared for such an important responsibility.

Make no mistake about it: When diagnostic gospel questions are asked lovingly, the Holy Spirit will communicate directly to the harvester through the response of the one being harvested. Our role as obedient ambassadors and fruitful harvesters is really not all that complicated, but it sure is exciting.

Shortly after the BAAAA card was developed, I was invited to speak at a weekend retreat in New Hampshire. The fall colors were magnificent and there was an enthusiastic group of 150 men from all over New England in attendance.

The receptivity of the group on Friday night was exceptional. Perhaps that was the reason the Lord prompted me to throw out the more formal presentation on Saturday. Instead, I gave everybody a 3x5 BAAAA card, some simple instructions and a strong challenge for each man to just ask those questions.

On Friday of the next week, I received a phone call from the retreat coordinator. Pastors had been calling in all week with reports of people coming to Christ. Several men had stopped and asked their unsaved friends the BAAAA questions on the way home from the weekend. It was encouraging to hear the coordinator say, "You know, Walter, that BAAAA thing really works!"

Dealing With "No" Answers

Something to keep in mind: As we ask these BAAAA questions, we don't necessarily want a yes answer. What we want is an *honest* answer. Actually, we should rejoice when we get a definite no because at least this enables us to pinpoint exactly where one of the problems is, and we can then ask permission to send clarifying written material. (In Appendix A there are four articles that may be used for this purpose. These easy-to-read articles have been prayerfully written in a language that non-Christians understand. Feel free to photocopy those pages for your own use.)

The fact that we simply ask permission to bring in an expert in the form of the printed page is frequently quite a surprise to our non-Christian friends. I particularly enjoy observing the reaction of people who say they are not willing to turn from sin. If in the past they have been lectured to about the consequences of their evil ways, they are shocked by this totally different response when someone doesn't scold or attempt to argue. It is very disarming.

Non-Christians are so accustomed to "religious" people trying to cram things down their throat that it is a great relief when it doesn't happen. Our non-confrontive action generally is appreciated, and, at times, even overwhelming. It is not uncommon for a non-Christian to say, "You're the *first* religious person I've ever met who doesn't insist on an argument." When we do non-confrontive harvesting, there is little opportunity for an argument, debate or even a hot discussion. What a refreshing change for all involved.

We will discuss the importance of follow-up procedures in future chapters, but, for now, I want to stress the idea of just *letting* someone say yes to those BAAAA questions. If the Holy Spirit has already done the preparation, the harvester must be careful not to put up road blocks. Instead, the harvester should continue going down the 3x5 card in order to let any receptive individual say yes to the diagnostic questions and say the simple prayer of commitment.

Because the appropriate Scripture reference is reproduced on the card, it is not necessary to use a Bible. Non-Christians will see the Scripture references, and most will realize that what is being asked comes directly from the Bible. If a harvester wants to use the Bible to locate each verse, it is all right to do so. The Word is powerful no matter how or where it is spoken.

Putting the Theory Into Practice

It's time to remind ourselves again exactly what we are doing. We must not forget that a large percentage of non-Christians are already ready. They are no longer non-Christians, but pre-Christians. Recognizing opportunities to participate in God's harvest fields needs to be a daily priority. Harvesting can be a natural activity that truly

changes our evangelistic thinking. We must remember too
that although God commands us to be His representatives
working in His harvest field the Holy Spirit has done all of
the preparation and is adequate to do any convincing that
may be necessary.

My all-time favorite harvesting experience happened shortly after the development of the BAAAA card. If
it had happened before that time, no doubt it would have
been a frustrating visit. Instead, it turned out to be one of
the easiest evangelism encounters I have experienced. At
the same time, it dramatically illustrated for me that stay-
ing with the diagnostic questions will allow someone who
has been prepared by the Holy Spirit to receive Christ.

It was my turn to take out two women from the
visitation group of my own church. We sent letters to homes
in the neighborhood and then called to set up a time to
make a brief visit. On this particular evening, we got an appointment with little trouble. After a good prayer time at
the church, we went to the home at the appointed time. We
were well received by a handsome middle-aged man. It took
little time for us to realize we were talking to a very sharp
and articulate defense lawyer.

He advised us that he had been a board member of
a church with a strong liberal reputation. He casually let it
be known that his church usually differed with the conser-
vatives, and that he didn't believe in this "born again" stuff.

In the first few minutes the stage was set. My heart
started to pound with excitement. The women looked nervous. I could tell they were praying hard.

"May I ask you a few questions about spiritual
things?" I said gently. He smiled and said, "Well, I usually
ask the questions but go right ahead."

I showed him the first question on my hand-held
visual as I asked, "Do you believe Jesus Christ died for you

on the cross and rose from the grave?" He weighed his words carefully and said, "Do you mean physically?" I smiled and said, "Yes. Do you believe His body actually rose from the grave?" He leaned back, looked up at the ceiling and said, "That's a good question. At our church we talk about the spirit being raised up, not necessarily the body."

Now, it's very important to realize there was no animosity in the room at this moment. In the first few minutes we were right down to bedrock fundamentals, but the atmosphere was relaxed. Thank God for the way He answered the prayers of those two women.

I purposely did not respond to his comment and after a short time that seemed interminable, I grinned and said, "Mr. Lawyer, you didn't answer my question."

He chuckled and said, "That's right, I didn't. Do I believe that Jesus Christ rose from the grave bodily. That's the question, right?"

"That's right," I said and kept quiet. (Big miracle!)

It must have been a full minute before he looked me straight in the eye and said, "Yes, I do. I believe that."

I wanted to cry out "Wow!" but instead I carefully went to the next BAAAA question. Several times, mostly out of habit, I suspect, he tried to avoid the questions by giving me various "stalls." Gently, I kept bringing him right back to BAAAA. The fascinating thing was that *he could not say no* to any of the direct BAAAA questions. Anything but a yes answer would have been perjury.

"Is there any good reason why you cannot say this simple prayer right now, aloud?" I asked.

He said, "No, I guess not." So, right there, in his own living room, he bowed his head and said, "Lord Jesus, I receive You as my Lord and Savior, Amen." This fine trial lawyer was ripe and didn't know it. We went through a brief follow-up procedure by showing him assurance verses. He agreed to read the Gospel of John and do a Bible study. Then came the icing on the cake. He said, with a sigh, "Well, I suppose this means that now *I'm* born again."

We *can* say with assurance that if he honestly and sincerely meant what he said in the presence of three human witnesses that night, he *is* born again and has the free gift of eternal life. It started as soon as he agreed in his heart with those five scriptural questions.

On occasion someone will express concern about the super-simple prayer. One reason it need not be long is that all the required doctrine is covered by God's perfect plan. Another important reason is that most non-Christians feel uncomfortable about any kind of prayer. Because we would like them to pray this prayer out loud, the more simple it is the easier it is for them. Again, we need to remember that for those brought up in an evangelical home, praying aloud is a way of life. The "Christianese" language we use when we pray seems very strange to a new or pre-Christian. While the prayers of commitment in some tracts are theologically strong, they tend to be strange or even some-what offensive to the bewildered pre-Christian.

So far, we have covered three of the four rather broad areas of the harvesting picture:

- Millions of pre-Christians are ready to be harvested.
- Millions of Christians refuse to harvest.
- Willing harvesters can pick ripe pre-Christians by simply asking five questions.

It is important to understand the problems and challenges in still another key area in order to complete the harvesting puzzle. We'll look at that in the next chapter.

E·I·G·H·T

Stalls and
Objections

*But a natural man does not accept the things
of the Spirit of God, for they are foolishness
to him, and he cannot understand them,
because they are spiritually appraised.*
—1 Corinthians 2:14

There I was, across the examining table from a congenial optometrist. It was obvious he loved to talk so he happily agreed to answer my questions as he went about the work of adjusting my glasses.

His answers were all affirmative until I came to "Do you agree to turn from sin?" He talked about the new morality which he openly practiced and said he just didn't want to turn from sin. I know it surprised him when I didn't react and criticize his loose morals. Instead, I thanked him for his honesty and asked permission to send him some information about sin that might possibly make him a happier person. He asked me to send it right away because in two weeks he was leaving to start a new job in Hawaii. As I left, he said, "Who knows? Maybe I'll turn over a new leaf. One of the main reasons I'm going to Hawaii is that

I'm not at all happy with myself."

Whenever we talk to people about Christ, various comments and questions will inevitably come up. We call these *stalls* and *objections*. While this kind of dialogue frequently sounds negative, it does not necessarily indicate that one is not ready to make a commitment to Christ. Therefore, it is important that we understand the real meaning of stalls and objections. Learning how to handle these situations is essential to avoiding needless controversy. It is a key part of the harvesting plan.

- An *objection* is a genuine reason that keeps a person from responding positively to God's offer of salvation.

- A *stall* is any comment or question that diverts a person away from and slows down the process of receiving Jesus Christ.

Shortly after we first introduced it, the Harvesting Seminar was attended by the senior district superintendent from one of the major denominations. This man of God has pastored many churches and is well known for his concern and love for evangelism. Many have since echoed the encouraging statement he made at that time: "Understanding the differences between stalls and objections and knowing how to handle them are the most helpful concepts I've ever learned in any evangelism training session."

Because the improper handling of stalls and objections seems to be a major reason why non-Christians are not being harvested, we would do well to take a closer look at what is involved in causing this to happen.

The Meaning of "Objections"

When a Christian starts talking to an unsaved person about spiritual things, the questions and comments frequently get more complicated and intense as the conversation progresses. Eventually, one of two things happens: Time runs out or, for one reason or another, the conversation gets bogged down. In both cases, Satan gets the victory.

Satan doesn't care how people don't come to Christ as long as they don't. The most effective way for Satan to accomplish this is to get a Christian to treat a stall like an objection and an objection like a stall. If Christians continue to do this, millions will put off taking the necessary steps to come to Christ. Yet it is conversely true that if our churches will equip harvesters to treat stalls and objections properly, millions will come to the saving knowledge of Jesus Christ.

It follows then that instructing believers to handle stalls and objections properly is certainly one of the most urgent jobs of the church.

First, let us concentrate on the objection. An objection, by our definition, is anything that directly interferes with the acceptance of BAAAA.

If to believe, admit, agree, acknowledge and accept (or its scriptural equivalent) is the way to come to Christ, the only way *not* to come to Christ is either not to be exposed to or to disagree with one or more of these five things.

A sincere no to any one of the BAAAA questions then is a sure sign that one is not yet ready to receive Christ. Because this is true, there are really only five objections. Only five things can keep one from receiving Jesus Christ:

1. I don't believe Jesus died for my sin and rose from the grave.

2. I don't admit I'm a sinner.

3. I don't agree to turn from my sin.

4. I don't acknowledge Jesus Christ as my Savior and Lord.

5. I don't accept God's free gift of salvation.

Recognizing an objection is easy when using the BAAAA card because an objection is a sincere no to any one (not necessarily all) of the questions. As previously suggested, the harvester should not overreact to a no but should say, "If I could give you information that would help you convince yourself that (whatever the objection is), would you read it?"

Usually, a pre-Christian will agree with this suggestion. Then it's just a matter of getting that specific information to them.

When the offer is made to send information and the subject is promptly changed, it generally is a relief to both parties. The pre-Christian is pleased that the Christian is not going to preach. The harvester feels good that a meaningless argument or vain discussion has been avoided.

It rarely happens, but if the pre-Christian indicates a desire to continue the spiritual discussion, the harvester just suggests that it would be preferable to do it after the article is read so that the discussion can be more meaningful. It also is appropriate to point out that as Christians, we do not claim to have all the answers. If the harvester receives permission to send information, he is allowed to bring in an authority on the subject. This minimizes the need for the harvester to be extra knowledgeable.

It is possible the pre-Christian may say no to the request to send information. If so, the harvester simply changes the subject to other things. But it shouldn't be a surprise if, at a later date, there is a request for the information.

By sending this written information, the harvester is being used by God to do some non-confrontive seed planting and watering in preparation for the harvest. The next step is to pray and wait patiently. Think of it in terms of a chess game. The first player makes a move and then must wait for the other player to make the next move.

Defining "Stalls"

Figure 4 is a list of the most common stalls, worded both in the form of a question and a comment. No doubt we could come up with a much longer list, but most additions would be variations of these twelve basic stalls.

For our practical purposes, a stall can be described as a way of trying to get around or avoid the main issue, God's perfect plan. Another way of looking at this is: An objection is a road block, but a stall is only a temporary detour.

The handling of stalls is simple and straightforward. A stall is usually one of two types: a question or a comment.

- **The question stall.** The easy, non-confrontive way to handle a question stall is to say, " I'm sorry, but I don't feel quite qualified to answer that."

- **The comment stall**. The easy, non-confrontive way to handle a comment stall is to say, "That's an interesting comment."

There is a third and remote possibility. Someone might insist that we personally answer or comment on their stall.

- **The insistent stall.** The easy, non-confrontive way to handle an insistent stall is to say, "May I come back to that in just a moment?"

After each and every stall, the harvester should always go back to BAAAA immediately.

Basic Stalls

1. Can you prove there is a God?/*You can't prove there is a God.*

2. What about people who don't believe in your God?/*Some non-Christians will certainly go to heaven.*

3. Do I have to believe in miracles?/*I don't believe in miracles.*

4. Is Christ the only way to God?/*I don't think Christ is the only way to God.*

5. Do I have to believe in heaven?/*I don't believe in heaven.*

6. Why do the innocent suffer?/*A loving God wouldn't allow innocent people to suffer.*

7. Isn't just believing too easy?/*Just believing seems too easy.*

8. Aren't Christians hypocrites?/*I think Christians are hypocritical and phony.*

9. Won't a good moral life get me to heaven?/*A good moral life will get me to heaven.*

10. Isn't the Bible full of errors?/*A lot of people say the Bible is full of errors.*

11. How much faith do you have to have?/*I don't have enough faith.*

12. Isn't Christian experience only psychological?/*Christian experience is only psychological.*

Figure 4

More often than not, when non-Christians make a comment stall, they are simply trying to get us to react. When we don't, it's generally perfectly acceptable to them.

After saying, "That is an interesting comment," we simply go back to the question at hand. As a variation, we could say, "Many people say that," or "Some people say that," or "I've never heard that before." Without agreeing with the stall, any one of these comments can be made in a rather complimentary way. We always go right back to BAAAA.

How about the question stall? Can we, in good conscience, say we don't feel qualified to answer a question? By all means. As a matter of fact, no one is qualified to adequately explain a stall to a non-Christian. First Corinthians 2:14 tells us why:

> The man without the Spirit does not accept the things of the Spirit of God, for they are foolishness to him, and he cannot understand them, because they are spiritually appraised.

According to this verse, no matter how eloquent we are in our explanation and no matter how brilliant the non-Christian, without the Spirit of God, it will all be foolishness. Now, this doesn't mean we should say, "You're a fool. You won't understand this." Instead, we more or less plead the Fifth Amendment and go right back to BAAAA.

This brings up an important question that needs to be addressed at this point. If 1 Corinthians 2:14 is true, how can *anyone* come to Christ? Are not the salvation verses also foolishness? This is one of the many theological enigmas that gets a lot of scholarly attention. It seems that God, through the divine intervention of His Holy Spirit, will allow anyone to understand BAAAA, or its scriptural equivalent, *but not much more.* If this were not so, no one would be able to come to Christ. How much more than BAAAA is a non-Christian able to understand before it all becomes "foolishness?" I don't know. Scripture does not tell us, but I believe it is safe to say, not much.

The insistent stall frequently is an emotional one.

One of the most heart-wrenching stalls is when a parent says, "I want you to tell me why your God allowed my child to die so tragically." With compassion, we can say, "That is really a tough one to answer. Could we come back to that in just a moment?" We go back to the BAAAA questions and finish them and then handle this insistent stall in the same way we handle an objection. We simply say, "If I could give you information that would help you understand why God allowed your child to die, would you read it?" We then copy some pages from a book or get a pamphlet on the subject from a Christian bookstore. By this action, we indicate that we would prefer to let an expert answer that question; again, that is generally accepted and appreciated.

Figure 5 has the text for another 3x5 card. Most harvesters find it helpful to keep this harvesting guide handy until each step of handling stalls and objections becomes familiar. If the card is read over and over again, it is readily committed to memory.

Harvesting Guide

To Open: *"May we talk about spiritual things?"*

The Gospel: *Gently ask the five BAAAA questions. (Show them the card and read the questions aloud.)*

| **Handling an Objection:** | *"If I could get you information that would help you convince yourself that (whatever the objection is), would you read it?"* |

Then Stop.

(Front)

Handling a Stall:	Comment — *"That's an interesting comment."*
	Question — *"I'm sorry, but I don't feel qualified to answer that question."*
	Insistent — *"Can we come back to that in just a moment?"*

Remember: *After every stall <u>don't stop</u>. Always go right back to BAAAA.*

Follow-up: *Carefully go over the back side of God's Perfect Plan.*

(Back)

Figure 5

Staying Away From Needless Controversy

My compulsion to understand and separate stalls from objections led to a new and interesting understanding of apologetics. Recently there has been a flood of excellent books that might be loosely classified as "practical apologetics for lay people."

The twelve stalls listed in *Figure 4* have been gleaned from several of these books and represent the most popular subjects discussed by the authors. Each book goes into considerable detail as to how one can explain these things to others.

What overwhelmed me was the fact that I did not need to know the answer to any one of these questions, or even be able to comment on these subjects, in order to help someone come to Christ. These things are of no immediate importance to the one who is harvesting or the one being harvested.

Now, before I am tarred and feathered by the irate Christians who love to study apologetics, let me quickly qualify what I am saying.

It is admirable for any Christian to understand and be able to explain these exciting subjects, but I feel they should be discussed with Christians only. Again, remember that 1 Corinthians 2:14 makes it very clear that talk of the Bible is foolishness to the non-Christian. Therefore, the only thing a harvester can really do is help a person understand the basic decisions necessary for a life-saving commitment.

There is absolutely nothing wrong with being knowledgeable, but it's a good idea for a harvester to use only a minimal amount of this knowledge when working in the harvest field. Otherwise, those being harvested may become confused.

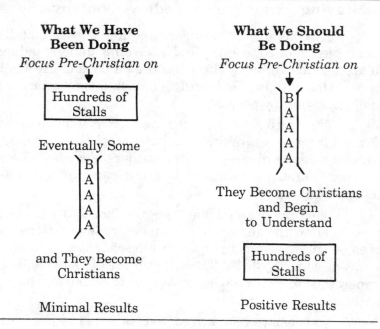

Figure 6

Please look carefully at *Figure 6*. The left side shows how we, fueled by our knowledge of apologetics, have engaged pre-Christians in conversations (hundreds of stalls). This diagram also suggests that we don't get to touchy subjects like BAAAA until everyone has been sifted through every conceivable stall.

The solution is to reverse this process completely. The right side suggests that we should immediately focus on the BAAAA questions. After the pre-Christian responds positively he then has the Holy Spirit who allows him to understand all truth.

At the start of this section, we suggested that the average Christian treats a stall like an objection and an objection like a stall. *Figure 6* illustrates this.

When an objection or a stall is treated as recommended, the harvester can handle it without confrontation and still see positive results. The systematic presentation of BAAAA along with the careful implementation of the stalls and objections procedure is key to successful non-confrontive harvesting.

N•I•N•E

Practice Makes Permanent

In all labor there is profit,
but mere talk leads only to poverty.
— Proverbs 14:23

During one of my first Harvesting Seminars, I had just completed enthusiastically listing many possible casual acquaintances people could share BAAAA with when a young man in the front row raised his hand. His question was simple (and devastating): "Mr. Bleecker, have you ever talked to *your* doctor about Jesus Christ?" I stood there before a group of fifty people and confessed, "No, I haven't . . . but yes, I will." And I did.

The medical plan I belong to uses a great variety of doctors; however, there is one doctor who gives me my yearly physical. I had never talked to him about the Lord. Because of the loving prodding of this young man, I realized there wasn't a good reason why I could not and should not practice what I preach.

Within a few months, it was time for that yearly physical. I went with the prayerful expectancy that the Lord would open up a door for me. During the visit, we came to a place that seemed to be appropriate, so I did exactly what I tell everyone else to do, I said, "Doc, could we talk about spiritual things?" He said, "Sure" and I almost fainted.

Because of his tight schedule, we decided to have the discussion over a relaxed lunch the following week. During the next few days I asked several of my faithful prayer warriors to say a few special prayers. The doctor and I met at a nice restaurant. Because I knew what his favorite sport was, I asked him about his last skiing adventure. With his usual enthusiasm, he told me about a great family ski trip and then said, "Wait a minute. I thought we were going to talk about spiritual things today."

Prayer works, doesn't it?

Again, I did exactly what I suggest everyone else do. I said, "Would it be okay if I asked you a few questions?" and he said, "Why certainly."

With a sensitive attitude, but in a direct way, I went right down the BAAAA card, asking all five questions. With minimal comment, he just gave me a genuine yes to every question. With some hesitation, he then bowed his head and said that child-like prayer aloud. I say "with some hesitation" because it was no doubt an unusual experience for him to pray out loud in a public place. I'm quite sure no one but the Lord and myself had any idea of what was happening at our table.

I felt like it, but I didn't jump and shout, "Hallelujah, the angels are rejoicing in heaven, Doc." Instead, I turned the card over and carefully went over each follow-up step (we will review these in a later chapter).

When we were done, he said, "You know, you really surprised me. I thought you were going to ask me to join your church or some religious group." He then said something that sent chills up my spine: "I've been a devout member of my church ever since I was old enough to remember, but you're the first person who has ever taken the time to explain this thing you call a personal relationship with Jesus Christ. I want you to know how much I appreciate that."

In Chapter 1, it was suggested that people are more open to talking about spiritual things today than at any other time in human history. Keeping this statement in mind will encourage us to be positive about the receptivity of the people God puts in our path. Of course, this does not mean *everyone* we meet will welcome us with open arms, but we can be assured we will get a receptive ear from most people, provided we approach them in a natural, non-offensive way.

Perhaps you are saying, "Okay, I'm convinced we should harvest, but I have a problem. I'm willing to talk to others about Christ, but I just don't have any non-Christian friends."

Because we have such different interests after becoming Christians, it is not uncommon to find our circle of close, non-Christian friends rapidly diminishing. The experts would like us to know, however, that if we are average, we have well over one hundred casual acquaintances:

- Business associates and clients
- Service clubs, 4-H
- Political organizations
- Athletic and musical activities
- Parent-teacher groups
- Boy and Girl Scouts
- Fraternal organizations
- Community groups and projects

- Gas station and restaurant owners
- Repair and maintenance people
- Cleaners, barbers, beauticians
- Retail business owners, clerks
- Insurance and travel agents
- Doctors, lawyers, dentists
- Investment advisors, bankers
- Neighbors
- And many more!

To be sure, many of these casual acquaintances are non-Christians. We already know these people either by name or at least by nodding acquaintance and we frequently have repeated contacts with them, so we have already "earned" the right to talk with them. Our casual acquaintances are our very best harvesting prospects and the easiest ones for non-confronters to talk with.

When is the best time to talk to a casual acquaintance? Any time we are with one is a good time. "Can't I just wait for my casual acquaintance to come to me and ask questions about spiritual things?" you may ask. That's just wishful thinking. It seldom happens.

Most of the time we are so busy filling our days with other matters that we just never get around to what's really important. It's not that there are few prospects; pre-Christians are everywhere. The greatest barrier to talking with the unsaved is that we just don't do it.

It is interesting to note that not once does the Bible mention unbelievers being invited or expected to come to church to hear the gospel. How did we ever get away from the biblical pattern? As Dr. Grubbs mentioned in the preface to this book: "We have inverted the [evangelistic] strategy from a 'go' to a 'come' structure."

First Corinthians 2:14 suggests that even if we do get a non-Christian to attend a church service, much of what is heard will seem foolish.

I'm certainly not recommending that we close our church doors to non-Christians. I am suggesting that the most important contribution a Christian can make does not only take place within the walls of a church building but also out there in God's harvest field where casual acquaintances are engaged in work, play and everyday activities.

An unusual thing happens when we start thinking about spiritual things in relation to the unsaved—we fear we will create a confrontation. You may have found yourself in a situation where each question or statement about Jesus Christ led to a more controversial question or statement until there was a disagreement or argument. When following the non-confrontive harvesting plan, this is not likely to happen.

Now, of course, it is possible to ask any question in an offensive way and make it sound confrontive. I cringe whenever I think of someone pointing a finger at a non-Christian and demanding, "Are you born again?" Harvesting is quite different from that. When we sensitively ask permission to ask someone a question about spiritual things, we can avoid confrontation if we graciously accept a yes or no answer without being judgmental.

Step by Step Through the Harvesting Process

The first step in a non-confrontive approach is to pray and remind ourselves to be calm and completely natural in manner and tone of voice. The next step varies from person to person. Some prefer to open the conversation by making a simple statement such as, "You know, I'm quite interested in spiritual things." A statement like this is usually casually acknowledged. This opens the way to ask, "May I ask you a question about spiritual things?"

A simple variation is to ask, "Would it be all right if we talk about spiritual things for a few minutes?" When there is an affirmative reply, we immediately ask permission to ask another question so that the non-confrontive questioning can continue.

One of my more enthusiastic pastor friends told me of still another approach. After experimenting, he came up with a very acceptable variation that fits his personality and style. He simply finds something in the conversation that enables him to say, "Oh, are you interested in spiritual things?" He seems to be able to find something spiritual in almost every sentence! Others have suggested lead-in comments such as: "You know, whenever I see you I feel a little guilty. I've known you for many years (months, weeks) and have never taken the time to talk to you about the most important thing we could possibly talk about—spiritual things."

How the transition is made is not important. What is important is that we always ask permission to ask another question.

If the casual acquaintance says no to our original question, our reply should be, "That's fine. I appreciate your honesty." Then we simply change the subject. There is no confrontation. But we shouldn't be surprised if at a later date the same casual acquaintance starts a spiritual discussion. It happens all the time. The vast majority of our casual acquaintances will gladly reply to our questions and the entire process will be non-threatening and non-confrontive. As we get into the habit of asking for permission to talk about spiritual things, we will discover so many people who are genuinely interested that we will not have to force ourselves on those who are not yet interested. What a relief to know that with grace and ease we can move ahead or back off as the Holy Spirit opens and closes the doors.

After receiving permission to proceed, we want to ask only questions that will draw out appropriate and honest responses. This is the sensitive and diplomatic way to find out exactly where the non-Christian stands, *without any pressure to change what they are presently doing or thinking.*

Most of us have some preconceived ideas about how long it takes to find out where a person is spiritually. In most cases, it need not take long at all. At this point in the conversation we do not have to explain the theology behind what is necessary for salvation. *The primary thing is to find out the individual's spiritual condition.* The best way to do this is to lovingly ask diagnostic questions.

We now come to a moment of truth. We cautiously remind ourselves that everything must be steeped in prayer, done in the power of the Holy Spirit and solidly based on Scripture. We have a biblical plan of salvation in the form of probing, non-threatening questions, which has been designed for equipping 90 percenters to harvest. When we combine this plan with the simple stalls and objections procedure, it becomes a virtually foolproof, non-threatening way to find out where someone is in relationship to Jesus Christ. Many casual acquaintances are willing to talk about spiritual things and are readily available. The best time to harvest is now because "now is the day of salvation" (2 Corinthians 6:2).

Why We Don't Harvest

At this point most Christians panic. Even though we are convinced that harvesting is truly non-confrontive, even though we sincerely believe that no Christian is exempt from talking about spiritual things, it is still the one thing we seem to fear and avoid at all costs.

I wish this were not so, but experience has borne this out repeatedly. No matter how enthusiastic and excited we are about the whole harvesting idea, it is much easier to talk ourselves out of it than to attempt it.

Again, one reason we do this is because of negative past experiences. We keep thinking about the time we got bogged down in meaningless discussions, or we said the wrong thing, or we just didn't know what to say.

Another reason is that we are just not familiar with the recommended responses. Even when the stalls and objections procedure is clearly understood, it is quite another thing to be able to react spontaneously to a question or comment according to those recommendations. To be able to give an immediate response to a stall, an objection or a comment *takes practice.*

Playing the "Harvesting Game"

How can we get practice without going through the embarrassment of falling flat on our face? No one likes to feel dumb. When we try to practice and experiment with something that is unfamiliar to us, that's exactly how we feel, and it can be mortifying.

One of the best ways to begin to solve this problem is through role play. It is essential to make this a carefully controlled, realistic activity. For some unknown reason, when Christians try to act like non-Christians they are usually completely unreasonable. Role play is like a laboratory experiment because we test, analyze and practice before going into the field. By playing a fun game we can bridge the gap between theory and actual on-the-job performance.

The game is played with cards or slips of paper that have one of the words *Believe, Admit, Agree, Acknowledge* or *Accept* on one side. On the opposite side is either a stall

or objection or permission to proceed. Each player has a
chance to let a hypothetical pre-Christian make a commitment to Jesus Christ. As the harvester asks the
pre-Christian the BAAAA questions, each player turns up
a "random comment" or "question" and responds for the
pre-Christian. The harvester must react with the correct
harvesting procedure. The group encourages, corrects and
occasionally lovingly razzes each harvester. (Complete
directions for "The Harvesting Game" are included in Appendix C.)

Experiences in the Harvesting Field

Reflecting back on the casual acquaintances I've
been privileged to talk to brings to mind a kaleidoscope of
people and places.

Writers of fiction could not come up with role play
stories as unique as those I have personally experienced.
No two dialogues are ever the same, but some of these experiences seem to typify the hundreds of responses I've had
to BAAAA.

When a television repairman came to our home, I
inquired if I could ask him a few questions about spiritual
things. He said, "Go ahead, you're paying for my time!"
After assuring him that he could work and talk at the same
time, I got right to it and asked if he believed that Jesus
Christ died on the cross and rose from the grave. Without
a bit of hesitation he said, "No, I don't believe that." His
reply was quick and definite. My equally candid response
was, "I appreciate your honesty and I imagine God does too.
If I could give you information that would help you convince yourself that Jesus Christ did die on the cross and
rise from the grave, would you read it?" "No," he said, "I
don't think I would."

I changed the subject immediately and watched as

he changed a small electronic part on the television set. He said I was lucky that he found and corrected the problem so quickly. As I was writing out a check for his modest bill, he said, "I suppose you're wondering why I was so hard on you when you asked me that religious question."

He went on to tell about his connection with a Unitarian group and how he believed that there are many ways to get to God and heaven. My parting comment to him as he went out the door was, "You know, that attitude isn't all bad. Perhaps sometime you'll take the time to discover how it only happens through Jesus Christ."

It seems to me that as a harvester, my obligation now is to pray that the Lord would put someone else into his path who would help him to do just that. I pray for him and others like him whenever I think of them.

A Successful "Fishing" Trip

When my son, Alan, turned seventeen, we took a long-planned trip to Alaska. Although our primary purpose was to fish for fish, we covenanted together to look for opportunities to fish for men also.

We fell in love with a fishing camp on a beautiful lake in British Columbia and made fast friends with the congenial owner. He was more than willing to give us all the inside information on how to catch the big ones. Over that inevitable cup of coffee, he asked what I did for a living. I looked at Alan, smiled and said, "I teach people how to ask questions." In a few minutes, we were right into the first question.

He hemmed and hawed and told of his church background as a member of a large, well-known church in Los Angeles. Finally he said, "I must be truthful. I'm just not sure I believe that Jesus rose from the grave." We promised to send him some information that would help clarify that for him and then promptly changed the subject back to fishing.

That day Alan caught the largest trout that either one of us had ever seen. Our friend told us it was two pounds heavier than the one that won the last fishing derby.

We left camp rejoicing over two very positive experiences. Within the next few days, we mailed our friend an article on the resurrection. Incidentally, when we arrived home, a warm thank you note was waiting. He had not only read the article but had already bought the book *More Than a Carpenter* by Josh McDowell[1] and was halfway through it.

Later we learned that this camp owner is actually a millionaire. He bought the camp for a lark; when he's there, he wants to be nothing more than a good fishing guide.

On the same trip, we had several other delightful harvesting experiences but none more dramatic than when we stopped at one of the friendly cafes along the Alcan Highway.

While eating at the counter, we noticed a young man sitting by himself at a corner table. We agreed he looked very troubled. "Shall we talk to him about the Lord?" I asked. Alan said, "Sure, go ahead, Dad. I'll pray." With my coffee cup as a security blanket, I walked over and said, "Have you been doing any fishing?" He said he had not but seemed reasonably willing to talk. I still can't believe I actually said this, but it just came out: "I haven't seen anyone look as sad as you in a long time." I know Dale Carnegie would agree that this is not the best way to win friends and influence people. I guess I said it in a caring way because he immediately looked up and said, "You're a Christian, aren't you?"

He went on to tell how he had gone forward at a crusade, attended church for awhile, but then quickly drifted away. I asked him what he did for a living. Without batting an eyelash, he said, "I rip people off." I could hardly believe what I was hearing as he described how he had become a professional thief and hated himself for it. That very morning he had stolen and sold some electrical equipment in order to buy the meal he was eating. "Are you going to turn me in?"

"Sure I am," I said. "I'm going to turn you in to God." It was the first time he smiled. I told him that in my opinion quite a few people "go forward" and do what someone suggests without making a genuine commitment to Jesus Christ. He agreed that this might have been what happened in his case. I assured him we could correct that but warned, "Let's not play games." By his expression, body language and attitude, I could tell he was relieved to talk to someone who seemed to understand what it felt like to use people as pawns.

He admitted to being a good con artist and confessed that he even tried to con God. I seldom do this, but because of the conversation, I jumped right to the "agree" step by saying, "Please be completely honest with me. Do you really want to stop ripping people off? Do you honestly want to try to turn away from *everything* God doesn't like?"

With big tears filling his eyes and a choked-up voice, he said, "Yes, I really do. Honest, I do."

About this time, Alan poked his head around the corner. He had taken a stroll outside and had been praying as hard as he knew how. I motioned for him to come over and we reviewed and amplified the front and back of the 3x5 card as a guide for this man's recommitment.

Right before our eyes, we saw a bitter, hardened thief turn into a soft little lamb as he said what he later called an "honest-to-God prayer." He promised to get in touch with a pastor friend of mine and attend his church.

Just like Philip and the Ethiopian eunuch, he went his way and Alan and I went ours. We rejoiced and prayed that this time this man honestly and sincerely meant what he said.

During that great vacation we experienced two things that were so special they seemed unreal. One day two of Jesus' disciples took a little time from their fishing trip to talk to a millionaire about the most important thing in the whole universe. Another day those same ordinary fishermen discussed the same revolutionary subject with a practicing, professional thief. Isn't God imaginative!

People Are Ready

One of the best examples of how easy it is to use BAAAA was a routine happening about a mile from my home. A new automotive repair facility opened in our town. On occasion, I would take my car there for servicing and repair. I got to know and enjoyed talking with John, the young manager. One morning when I took my car in, I asked if we could talk about spiritual things. He said he would like that very much. We agreed to have coffee when I picked up the car at 3:00 o'clock.

When I arrived, John said he was very sorry but he just couldn't leave the shop. Several people were out sick, and he had to stay there to answer the phone. I was ready to say I'd come back some other time but before I could say it, he said, "Why can't we just talk right here in the shop?" Why not, indeed. I prayed silently that the phone wouldn't ring — and it didn't.

The noise and confusion that surrounded us didn't stop him from saying yes to those five straightforward questions either. Yes, in a way, it did seem unusual to be talking about spiritual things while standing at a service desk in a busy garage. Actually, what happened there could be a natural and normal daily experience for every Christian.

You see, the Holy Spirit had already done the work in John's heart and in the hearts of the others previously mentioned. That's why, even in unusual surroundings, John bowed his head without any hesitation, and received Jesus Christ as Lord and Savior.

In a few weeks, John publicly reconfirmed his commitment to Jesus Christ and joined a church. Today, after almost two years, John and his wife are both teaching Sunday school and the whole family is actively involved in church and are growing like beautiful flowers.

Hopefully the harvesting experiences I've shared with you demonstrate that what is recommended here is unbelievably simple and, at the same time, very effective.

It took no talent, special ability or spiritual gift for me to interact with these very different people. In each case, I was able to discover where each one was in relationship to Jesus Christ. All that was required was the presence of mind to prayerfully follow the instructions, and that comes only with practice.

1. Josh McDowell, *More Than a Carpenter* (Wheaton, IL: Tyndale House Publishers, 1977).

T • E • N

Ripe Fruit
or Rotten?

*He who has the Son has the life; he who does not
have the Son of God does not have the life.*
— 1 John 5:12

It was early Sunday morning. I was driving coast to coast
with the luxury of some extra time to enjoy our great
country. Sunday morning is a wonderful time to gawk at
cities without fighting traffic congestion, so I headed to the
downtown area of a major midwestern city.

At breakfast time, I checked the yellow pages for a
church to visit. A large, right-on evangelical church caught
my eye. It had two morning services and two Sunday school
sessions. As I was having a relaxed breakfast, it occurred
to me that this would be a good time for an experiment. For
a long time I had been tempted to try something when visiting a church for the first time, and this was the perfect
opportunity!

I was middle-aged when I made my commitment to
Jesus Christ. Although I was reasonably well educated, I
was pitifully ignorant of the Bible. Because of this, I experienced many feelings of inadequacy that made me very

uncomfortable when I first attended adult Sunday school and Bible study. The spirit was willing but during any biblical teaching situation, I just felt dumb.

With these thoughts in mind, I confess I had a hidden desire to put this church on the spot. I arrived just in time for the first Sunday school session. The lobby of the sanctuary was a beehive of activity. Spotting someone who looked "official," I said,"Could you please tell me where a new Christian would go to Sunday school?" He looked somewhat surprised and said, "I'm really not sure. Please wait right here for a minute." He returned promptly and took me directly to a room filled with people my own age. I was introduced and warmly welcomed.

Just what I expected happened. For the next hour, a most erudite middle-age man did a very good job of dissecting verses in the book of Hebrews. There was some participation from the group, but this usually consisted of some carefully worded questions or comments.

I thought back not too many years before when I was physically mature but spiritually a baby. If I had walked into this class then, almost all of what I was hearing would have gone right over my head. Even though most of the others in the group could understand the theological language being used, a new Christian might easily be turned off, if not completely overwhelmed.

I have since visited many churches and it makes no difference if they are large or small, rural or urban. Most churches simply don't have many new Christians so they don't bother with a Sunday school class for them. If a new Christian does come along, he is frequently included in a "new members'" class, but these classes are usually attended by people who have recently moved and have been active in another church. What normally goes on in a new members' class, and in most adult Sunday school classes, can be threatening to someone coming in as a brand new Christian, especially if that person is unchurched. Even the church service itself is foreign to anyone not brought up in the evangelical tradition.

We've found that using "Discovery Groups" has helped us to solve this problem. Discovery Group is our name for a small discussion and informal Bible study group designed especially for new Christians. A well-planned Discovery Group becomes a "half-way house" that bridges the gap between the unchurched and the evangelical tradition for a new believer.

The Discovery Group

A Discovery Group get-together can be tailor-made for those who have little biblical knowledge and are ashamed to admit their lack of biblical knowledge. Small group meetings can be held either in a home or at the church. A favorite meeting time is just prior to the worship service at church.

Below you'll find some simple guidelines for a successful Discovery Group:

1. Members can come without going to the worship service. (Once they are there, they frequently go anyway.)

2. Keep the meetings very informal. (A living room-type setting is recommended.)

3. Serve homemade cinnamon buns!

4. Participation is voluntary. (No one is called on.)

5. It is always acceptable to come and just listen.

The Discovery Group is an excellent place to plug in the unchurched. It makes them feel welcome and involved without the pressure to join the church or go to a

Sunday school class where they may feel uncomfortable.

When we first started a group at my own church, we were fortunate to have a backlog of people who were physically mature adults but "babes in Christ." We also had a deacon who caught the vision and joyfully took on the project. A successful group must be led (not taught) by someone who not only thoroughly understands its real purpose, but also is very sensitive.

Rich and his wife, Shirley, enthusiastically put together a small group of new believers. Over an eight-week period, this diversified group congealed beautifully. What a thrill to watch a somewhat confused group come alive and develop confidence in spiritual things and their knowledge of the Bible. Most of the participants of that group are now active in our church and are vital church members.

Personal Follow-Up

Yet no matter how successful a Discovery Group program is, it is still urgent that every new Christian be personally followed up. Follow-up needs our concentrated attention. Like some other well-known evangelism terms, it is often misunderstood or used as a catch-all phrase. False commitments are usually blamed on lack of follow-up, even if it has nothing to do with the problem.

We will first look at what should be done immediately after a genuine commitment is made. Then we will examine some reasons for false commitments and how they can be minimized.

The Big "If"

Follow-up should start the minute someone receives Jesus Christ—and it never ends.

How to best help a new believer is a touchy area because each individual is unique. Each one has a varying capacity and willingness to grow. We, as Christians, also go about this work with varying degrees of intensity, depending on our past experiences, temperament and willingness to be of service.

Our job as harvesters should be to see that this growth process gets started and then share the responsibility with others. We need to encourage and edify immediately but, at the same time, be careful not to overwhelm the new Christian.

The back of the BAAAA card (*Figure 7*) will help us to do just that.

If you honestly and sincerely said yes to those five questions and meant it in your heart (Romans 10:9), then you have the assurance of eternal life (1 John 5:11-13).

Some Important Things For You To Do:

1. Read your Bible to discover God's message for you (2 Timothy 3:15-17).

2. Talk to God in prayer often about yourself and others (Philippians 4:6,7).

3. Develop a lifestyle consistent with Bible principles (1 John 2:6).

4. Tell others about Christ in your own way (Acts 1:8).

5. Take the initiative to faithfully attend a Bible-teaching church for worship, fellowship, growth and service (Hebrews 10:24,25).

Figure 7

The first sentence on the back of this card starts with a big *if*. It is urgent that the significance of this *if* be made clear to the newly committed Christian *and* to every harvester. The responsibility for the consequences of this *if* is directly on the individual believer and God Himself.

If a pre-Christian honestly and sincerely says yes to the five questions and genuinely means it, then he:

- has the Holy Spirit;
- is born again;
- has a personal relationship with Jesus Christ;
- has the free gift of eternal life; and
- will develop a deep hunger and thirst for righteousness.

If, on the other hand, a pre-Christian did not honestly and sincerely mean what he said, then, according to 1 John 5:10-12, he does not have any of these things because just saying a prayer does not save him:

> The one who believes in the Son of God has the witness in himself; the one who does not believe God has made Him a liar, because he has not believed in the witness that God has borne concerning His Son. And the witness is this, that God has given us eternal life, and this life is in His Son. He who has the Son has the life; he who does not have the Son of God does not have the life.

An honest mental and heart commitment to Jesus Christ must be made. For this reason it is important that harvesters slow down here and carefully discern the individual's sincerity level. This requires some tact on the part of the harvester. It would be wrong to doubt a pre-Christian's sincerity, but at the same time it is important to make sure he or she has not said yes just to please the harvester. In any event, it is the harvester's responsibility to emphasize the statement, "*If* you honestly and sincerely said yes . . . " No one ever has the authority to say, "You're saved," "You're born again," or "You're a Christian now." But we do have the right and joy of saying, "*If you honestly and sincerely said yes to those five questions, then you can positively know these things.*" We must always put the responsibility for the decision squarely on the one coming to Christ and on the Holy Spirit. We need to stress this with every believer and make sure that every harvester understands it, too. There are only two people who know for sure if a Christian is truly saved — the individual Christian and God.

Follow-Up Doesn't Have to Be Complicated

There are many ways to encourage a brand new Christian. In *Figure 7* you'll find a few simple suggestions that are a good place to start. They stress the importance of Bible study, prayer, a Christian lifestyle, sharing the good news and church involvement.

A simple Bible study in the Gospel of John will help a new Christian see the overall picture of salvation and assurance. I like to think of the Gospel of John as a summary of what Christianity is all about. We recommend that all new Christians read the entire Gospel of John several times (at least once in a modern language translation) and then do a simple Bible study, like the one in Appendix B.

Arrangements should be made for someone to meet for about an hour with the new believer. It makes good sense to match up a new Christian with an appropriate follow-through person. Women should work with other women, men with other men and couples with couples. A Bible, a completed Bible study and a copy of the BAAAA card usually trigger an active discussion.

The follow-up person should be careful not to overwhelm the new believer at this point. This is why we suggest starting with a one-hour session. In this session, every attempt should be made to fold the new believer into a Bible-believing church.

How's Your Follow-Up?

When it comes right down to it, any church can have a good, sensitive follow-up program. There is certainly no shortage of appropriate material. Christian bookstores have all kinds of excellent studies for new Christians in any stage of growth.* We do not need to worry about finding good material. We do need to commit ourselves to follow-up and help each other implement the materials available. We should do everything possible to encourage and challenge each other to grow.

The Problems of False Commitments

False commitment has plagued every evangelistic effort since the Lord ascended to heaven. Satan specializes in this area. He loves to work in the gray areas of confusion. He will do everything in his power to get a false commitment from someone who is considering the plan of salvation. My experience has shown that Satan often uses naive Christians to help him accomplish his dastardly deeds.

The following scenario will be familiar to most readers. It could take place in any kind of an evangelistic endeavor, although it is dramatically evident in crusade efforts. After much preparation and prayer, a strong biblical invitation is given, and in some way people respond to the gospel message. These slightly nervous and open-hearted people are usually counseled by a most sincere, dedicated

---

* Campus Crusade for Christ's *Transferable Concepts* and the *Ten Basic Steps* are excellent follow-up booklets, covering subjects from assurance of salvation to prayer. These booklets are available at your local Christian bookstore, or order directly from Here's Life Publishers.

Christian. The counselors are trained to use some excellent materials, and with enthusiasm they take the individuals through various passages of Scripture and a prayer of commitment. Then, a review of what has just happened takes place.

Those of us who have come to Christ in our adult years know that the one coming to Christ goes through many mental and emotional flip-flops. At this very crucial time, pre-Christians are frequently confused; some don't even clearly remember what they have just done. The counselors, wanting to be sensitive, go over what actually happened from their own perspective instead of letting the pre-Christians share their experience. This can cause even more confusion because we all react in such different ways.

Sensing the need to terminate, the counselors conclude the interview with some variation of: "Congratulations, you're saved! You're a Christian now." Of course, in some cases it is true. Many come to the saving knowledge of Jesus Christ in just this way. But for others the glow wears off and nothing develops. There is no growth, no change and no desire for the Word.

What I am suggesting is that it is possible for a non-Christian to participate in some recommended activities, even say a prayer, and still not receive Christ.

We have all heard the sad statistics which indicate that a huge percent of those making a commitment never develop in their relationship with the Lord. For whatever reason, the decision did not "take." These discouraging reports have baffled church leaders for years. What happens? What goes wrong? Is the wrong plan used? Should more time be spent on bringing up and answering troublesome questions? Should the follow-up materials be improved?

Pinpointing the Problem

Let's try to put our finger on where the problem lies. If a person makes a sincere biblical commitment, the life of God is immediately implanted within that person through the action of the Holy Spirit. As a result, there will be a hunger and thirst for righteousness; there will be a desire to grow closer to the Lord Jesus Christ; and there will be some evidence of change.

If a person does not make a sincere biblical commitment, the life of God is not implanted in that individual. There will not be a substantial hunger or thirst for righteousness or a strong desire to grow closer to the Lord or any real evidence of change.

So where does the problem of a false commitment come from? There are several possibilities:

- The plan of salvation was not accurate or complete; therefore, it was not in accordance with Scripture.

- The scriptural plan of salvation was misunderstood by the one trying to come to Christ.

- The scriptural plan of salvation was incorrectly presented by the Christian.

- The one coming to Christ was less than completely honest when making his decision.

There are really no new solutions in this troublesome area, but these recommendations may help to minimize the problem:

- Clearly present a simple but complete scriptural plan of salvation.

- Discover those not ready to come to Christ and sensitively identify their real objections.

- Help the ones who have been prepared by the Holy Spirit to come to Christ and understand the simplicity of receiving Jesus Christ as Savior and Lord.

- Place the responsibility for the sincerity of the commitment on the one making the commitment and on the Holy Spirit.

- Make a concerted effort to follow through with every person making a commitment.

Before leaving the subject of sincere commitment, let's look at another touchy area.

Church People but Not Christians

Over the years as I have presented God's perfect plan to those established in the church, there have been some very revealing reactions. In one seminar I was particularly emphatic about repentance and the need for a pre-Christian to sincerely want to turn from sin. Somewhere along the way I made a remark to the effect that committed Christians must not and, in fact, do not purposely sin. After the meeting, a young man I'll call Fred came up and as soon as we were alone he said, "What you said bothers me because there are certain things I'm doing that I know God doesn't like. Frankly, I'm not willing to turn away from them."

Now, this did not really shock me, but it did cause me to weigh my words. As we continued, he voluntarily told me of an occasional involvement he was having with a woman other than his wife.

Being extra-sensitive is not one of my strong points, so, after a quick prayer for wisdom, I lovingly said, "Let me get this straight. Is this something you plan? Do you purpose to do this?"

"Not often," he replied, "yet I'm certain God doesn't like what I'm doing. But everyone slips once in awhile."

Sensing his openness and sincerity, I quickly sent up another prayer, took a deep breath and said, "Fred, if you're a committed Christian, you cannot plan and purpose to do something you know God forbids."

"I know I shouldn't," he replied sheepishly, "but like I said, everyone slips."

"That's right. I agree. Everyone slips. But a Christian must never plan and schedule sin."

As you might imagine, the conversation was becoming tense. With a trace of anger in his voice, he said, "Are you trying to say I'm not saved?"

Fortunately, I had enough practical experience to know I should back off. With as much compassion as I could muster, I said, "No, I'm not. I would never presume that. But if any Christian regularly plans to sin, it would be wise for him to examine his commitment to the Lord Jesus Christ."

There was a long silence before two moist eyes looked straight into mine. "I've been concerned about this BAAAA thing," Fred admitted. "I'm not sure I did all those things when I went forward five years ago. I said a prayer all right, but maybe I didn't mean what I prayed. I'm not sure."

This man had made a sincere, but incomplete or confused, commitment. I recommended he make a recommitment. For a split second I thought I was going to receive a punch in the nose, but the threat disappeared almost as soon as it surfaced. He agreed he needed to examine his relationship with the Lord, but he wanted to reflect on our conversation. He thanked me profusely for talking with him.

Within the next week, Fred and his pastor got together for lunch. In the privacy of his car, he honestly and sincerely said yes to God by once and for all agreeing to a carefully worded biblical plan of salvation in the presence of his pastor.

I believe our evangelical churches are spotted with people just like Fred. They are nice people who are hanging around the church thinking they are Bible-believing Christians because someone told them they were saved. There is no question about the fact that they said a prayer and/or went forward. Unfortunately, in many cases, they are not at all sure of what they said because they were somewhat confused at the time.

If we would dare to talk openly with them, we would probably learn that they have little or no desire to read the Bible. They are, in fact, bored by biblical teaching but go along with Sunday school and church because it just seems to be the thing to do. We would probably be shocked to discover that some of these intelligent people are fuzzy when it comes to assurance of their salvation and what they really believe.

I'm certainly not recommending we start a witch hunt, but when we do locate these folks, we should carefully and sensitively take them through BAAAA as a recommitment.

A Final Thought

As we attempt to follow up new believers, we should be aware of one other area of caution. Our natural tendency is to automatically assume that anyone coming to Christ will go through the same or similar experience we went through. Of course, this is not so. Just as no two people ever come to Christ in exactly the same way, no two people grow in Christ in exactly the same way. Because of this, we can expect differences in growth patterns.

I like to think of new Christians as firecrackers. Some have short, dry fuses that go off immediately with a big bang. Others have longer, wet fuses that seem to take forever to go off. Yes, we can expect change, but we must be patient. Sometimes it takes a little longer than we would like. Where there is a genuine commitment, God always does His part and creates the desire to grow.

E·L·E·V·E·N

Community Harvesting

Go therefore and make disciples of all the nations.
— Matthew 28:19

Everyone warned us—Pennsylvania is a tough state. Pastor after pastor commented that people in that particular part of the country are not open to talking about spiritual things.

I'll never forget the first night my wife and I worked with a handful of people in a small, struggling church on the outskirts of Scranton, Pennsylvania. They had followed our recommended procedure by sending out letters to the neighbors in ever-widening circles around the church. The letter simply said, "Someone from the visiting committee will be calling for an appointment for a brief visit. We'd love to get to know you." Just two weeks after the mailing we started calling. A man answered our first telephone call and said, "I'm sorry, but we're busy tonight. Perhaps some other time." We got a negative response to the next call. On the third phone call a woman answered and said, "I'd love to have you stop by. I'm right across the street from the church, you know." The mouths of those on the harvesting

116

team dropped open in surprise. The pastor beamed. My wife, an elder and his wife spent a delightful forty-five minutes with this charming lady. She responded positively to BAAAA and made a commitment to Jesus Christ. She said she was an inactive member of another church but enthusiastically agreed to read the Gospel of John, do a Bible study and meet regularly with the elder's wife.

The pastor commented, "Isn't this ridiculous? We have waved at and greeted this lady over the years, yet no one has ever taken the time to talk to her about Jesus Christ."

Each chapter of this book has stressed that every Christian, in addition to being a good example (witness), must be involved in helping those whom God has already prepared come to the saving knowledge of Jesus Christ.

Where does successful harvesting begin? With the enthusiasm of Christian leaders. Sadly, it seems that most Christian leaders (I'm referring to the lay leadership in the church) have never personally brought someone to Christ. And what is even more tragic is that the same leaders have done a super job of convincing each other that this is perfectly acceptable. On top of that, it is unreasonable to expect others to do something as urgent as harvesting if the leaders are not personally willing to do it.

The scope of this book does not allow for in-depth observations about church leadership, but two things need to be pointed out. First, leadership in a church is different from most other organizations. Even though the leaders may be capable and conscientious in certain areas of their ministry, the fact that they are *volunteers with limited accountability* impacts their actions.

My observation is that Christian leaders seldom challenge others to do one-on-one evangelism because they are not doing it themselves. Rather than being held accountable for their failure to evangelize, the leaders are just excused with no recourse whatsoever. When Christians in the local church observe that their leaders prefer not to do one-on-one evangelism, they also don't do it.

When church members and church leaders refuse to do what is commanded by Scripture, usually nothing happens at all. Because of the obvious lack of enforceable accountability, a motivating factor in the business world, the secular chain-of-command does not work effectively in the church.

The second point to be looked at is that a smoothly run organization depends on accurately identifying its leaders. Often the church leaders are assumed to be those on the board, the committee chairmen and those in prominent positions. Many pastors are shocked to learn who the active people of the church actually look to for leadership. Few churches know who their *real* leaders are.

To soften the whole chain-of-command concept, I prefer to use the phrase "lineal leader ladder." In this context, *lineal* simply means ascending or descending in a direct line.

Every church already has a lineal leader ladder. The way to determine exactly who is on each step of the ladder is to ask the ones being led.

To assist in accomplishing this, a church may want to distribute a leadership questionnaire (*Figure 8*) to active church members through known activity channels, including Sunday schools and Bible studies but not at a church service.

When the results are tabulated, a very clear picture will evolve of who the active people in the church perceive to be their leaders. The leaders may not be the ones listed on the church roster, but they are those whom the people in the church look to for direction.

Leadership Identification Questionnaire

Your Help Is Needed

Please take the necessary time to fill out this leadership questionnaire. The results will be used to help shape future programming for the church. It has been given only to those who are currently involved in activities of this church (other than the worship service).

1. If the pastor and/or staff were not here, to whom would you look for leadership in our church?

   _____

2. Now write in the names of your next five choices of whom you would look to for leadership. (Don't be modest. If you see yourself as a leader, include your name.)

   _____

   _____

   _____

   _____

   _____

3. Place your unsigned list in the box provided at the back of the church.

Figure 8

It is impossible to establish evangelism as a way of life in a local church if the pastor and staff and those lay leaders at the top of the lineal leader ladder do not accept responsibility to regularly pick the ripe fruit that God has commanded us to harvest. Therefore, challenging the lineal leader ladder to do harvesting may be the most urgent project at hand.

Involving the Leadership in Harvesting

Starting with the pastor and the top of the lineal leader ladder, leaders must be encouraged and motivated to start practicing harvesting at their own pace. Two ways to accomplish this are through *bite-size challenges* and *voluntary accountability*. Because each of us is unique, it is important to encourage leaders to individually determine their own appropriate bite size and time frame for their personal God-oriented challenge.

As these leaders involve themselves in a harvesting project, expectations must be specific but, at the same time, flexible enough to fit busy schedules — not some preconceived timetable.

Each leader is helped to decide individually what can be willingly accomplished over what period of time. This is not a one-time crash program. Remember, the objective is to alter lifestyles to include harvesting as an on-going priority. This requires more than methodology and knowledge. It requires challenge, practice and practical application as well, as illustrated by the following story.

Right up until the short illness before her death, my mother-in-law was extremely active. For more than eighty years she participated in everything imaginable except one thing. She never learned to drive a car. In her lifetime, she no doubt watched hundreds of different people drive. At one point, someone even gave her a gift of driving lessons. She attended the classroom instruction and watched several movies, which she thoroughly enjoyed. She did everything in that driving school except one thing. She refused to get behind the wheel of a car. If she had lived to be 180 years old, attended every driving school and read every book ever published about driving, she would still never become a driver until she actually got behind the wheel and drove.

By the same token, a Christian leader can spend an entire lifetime giving personal testimony, encouraging others to do evangelism and attending evangelism seminars, but not lead a single person to the Lord. In order to be a harvester, one must *pick* that which is ready to be harvested. In order to help someone come to the saving knowledge of Jesus Christ and encourage others to do the same, one must not only *know* how to harvest but one must also *do* it.

Accountability as Part of the Harvesting Plan

The word *covenant* is not foreign to Christians. It is simply an agreement between persons. In harvesting we use a specialized definition: "A solemn compact between members of a church to maintain its disciplines." In order to get the church active in God's harvesting field, church members need to be encouraged to participate in three covenants.

A One-Time Harvesting Covenant

One person agrees to present BAAAA to a casual acquaintance and is voluntarily accountable to another who also agrees to share BAAAA with someone. They must both sign the following covenant.

As God provides the opportunity, I will attempt to use BAAAA to harvest at least one of my casual acquaintances within the next seven days. I will pray for a similar divine appointment for my harvesting partner. We will give an account of the experience and constructively critique one another by phone or in person before one week from today.

Signed _____

Date _____

A Two-Time Harvesting Covenant

Harvesting partners take turns presenting BAAAA

to casual acquaintances over breakfast or lunch. One partner invites an unsaved casual acquaintance to have breakfast or lunch with the two of them. The guest is always told that spiritual things will be discussed. Some time during the meal one harvester presents BAAAA. At another breakfast or luncheon meeting with a different casual acquaintance, the roles are reversed. The harvesters get together and constructively critique each other. They both sign the following covenant:

> As God provides the opportunity within the next month, I will make a breakfast or luncheon appointment with one of my non-Christian casual acquaintances to meet with my harvesting partner and myself. I will pray for a similar divine appointment for my partner. I agree to attempt to use BAAAA to harvest one of these guests, to pray for my harvesting partner and to have an evaluation session when the two appointments have been completed.
>
> Signed _____
>
> Date _____

The Community Harvesting Plan

The Five-Time Harvesting Covenant is an opportunity for every leader to see experienced harvesters present BAAAA and demonstrate the stalls and objections procedure several times. It's called the *Community Harvesting Visitation Plan*. In addition to providing invaluable personal experience, it also demonstrates how to teach others to harvest according to the 2 Timothy 2:2 model. Paul said:

> And the things which you have heard from me in the presence of many witnesses, these entrust to faithful men, who will be able to teach others also (2 Timothy 2:2).

All of the training for community harvesting is done

by leaders who have themselves completed the harvesting covenants. Five specific dates are set well in advance and arrangements are made for each new 90 percenter to observe five different harvesting attempts. This is usually done over a one- to three-month period.

The group is always made up of three people: two women and one man or two men and one woman. Letters, on church stationery, are sent out to neighbors, in ever-widening circles around the church. These letters are mailed well in advance of each visitation date. They state that someone from the church will be phoning to arrange for a brief, neighborly visit. On the appointed evening, phone calls are made and a short visit is arranged for that same evening. During the friendly conversation, permission is requested to ask a few questions. If there is a positive response to the questions, harvesting occurs. If there is a negative response, permission is requested to send information. If neither occurs, the short social visit is enjoyed by all. It's just that simple.

To see how the community harvesting plan is working within one Wyoming church, I'd encourage you to read Appendix D, "Let the Harvest Happen," an article by Pastor Michael Huber which appeared in his denominational publication.

Accomplishing the Goal of Community Harvesting

The community harvesting plan has a very different purpose from other visiting programs. Its real purpose is to provide practical harvesting experience for 90 percenters. The plan should not be used to replace other visitation programs. Visitation of the sick and needy should be done by those with the spiritual gift of mercy. Friendly visitation, with no planned agendas, can still be done by anyone, anytime.

We must be careful not to overlook our faithful 10 percenters here. There are many wonderful opportunities for this small group of enthusiastic saints. They can be organized to make visits on the non-Christian parents of the children in Sunday school and the unsaved relatives of church members. These spiritually gifted "evangelists" are ideal for making calls on first-time visitors. Ten percenters should be constantly encouraged to do all kinds of creative evangelism (rest homes, county fairs, rescue missions, street evangelism, etc.).

Community harvesting is designed to complement and supplement all other types of visitation. It reaches those who are seldom, if ever, contacted by any other group. It can go on simultaneously with all other visitation efforts.

The Community Harvesting Visitation Plan has a double guarantee: If the plan is faithfully followed as recommended, it is guaranteed to work and will perpetuate itself. If the lineal leader ladder refuses to participate, it is guaranteed to fail. This has been proven repeatedly.

As a result of my work in community harvesting, I've been involved in some interesting situations over the years.

About ten years ago we moved. After getting fairly established in our new Bible church, I convinced the pastor to allow me to demonstrate the plan to him. We followed the usual procedure. I sent out letters to those immediately surrounding our church.

Two weeks later, the pastor and I were getting ready to make the phone calls. He said, "Oh, you shouldn't have sent a letter to Darlene and Glenn Cobb. They live right next door to the church. She's a Christian and her husband is not. I've already talked to him. Let's try someone else." Now, I don't usually argue with my pastor but because the letter had already been sent, I got him to let me at least make the phone call. We were both surprised when Darlene answered the phone and said, "I'm so glad you called. My husband wants you to come." Talk about ripe fruit. In the comfort of his own living room, Glenn Cobb received Jesus Christ as his Lord and Savior. Today, Glenn, Darlene and their two daughters are one of the most active families in our fellowship.

No Place Too Small

Maine is without a doubt one of my favorite places. We own a little cabin on a lake, almost in the center of that great state. Several years ago it was a thrill for me to try the harvesting plan with the fun-loving part-time pastor of the local Bible church.

The first thing he said, in his Maine accent, was, "Telephone thing won't work heah."

"Why not?" I chided.

"Well, I know everbody in town. They'll laugh at me if I say something like that."

"Let's just tell them we're planning on visiting *everybody* in town," I said.

This was a typical telephone conversation:

"Hello, Maggie?"

"Eh, ya!"

"This is Fred Williams over at the church."

"Oh, shuah! How are ya, Fred?"

"Maggie, we've decided to make a brief visit on every family in town. Can we come over tonight or would some other time be bettah?"

"Come right over. I'll put the coffee on!"

But what do you do when you run out of families?

Well, there are always people in the next town!

No Place Too Odd

Paul Rowan is an elder who has faithfully led community harvesting in my church. His favorite visit is the one he made on a beautiful spring evening. When he phoned for the appointment, a woman's voice said, "You're welcome to come, but I'll be around back with the animals." When the harvesters arrived, they found a lovely house with a trim barn behind. Sure enough, the woman was standing in the middle of six goats. She greeted Paul warmly and said, "I can talk to you while I'm milking the goats if you don't mind." The harvesters chuckled and explained the "sheep" plan and went right into asking the BAAAA questions. It may not have been a very pious setting, but the harvesters all agreed — the atmosphere had no effect on the sincerity of the woman's answers.

No Place Too Difficult

The pastor of a large church in Atlanta, Georgia, was pleased with the response of his people to the Harvesting Seminar held at his church. It was encouraging to hear him speak so positively about it during the Sunday services. On Monday, as we were getting ready to experiment with the community harvesting project, he was less enthusiastic.

"We sent out the letters in our neighborhood just as you instructed, but we have a problem," he said. He went on to explain that almost all of the immediate neighbors around the church were Jewish. He was guessing the response would probably be poor.

"Why should it be?" I said as I mustered up my positive attitude. "After all, we just want to pay them a friendly visit." We prayed and I picked up the phone to make the first telephone call to a home right down the street. A woman answered, and sure enough, her heavy Jewish accent could not be mistaken.

"Could we come by for a brief visit?" I asked cheerfully.

"Would it make any difference to you that I'm Jewish?" she queried.

"Of course not," I replied.

"Come along then. I'd be happy to see you."

I thought the pastor would faint from shock. "I can't believe it," he said with bewilderment. I agreed.

He and I and one of the women from the church had a wonderful visit with this charming widow who had lived in the neighborhood for years. As we lovingly presented the gospel, she understandably had some doubts about Jesus Christ. We asked for and received permission to send information that would help her convince herself that Jesus is, in fact, the Messiah.

To this day, the pastor is not completely convinced that I didn't set the whole thing up ahead of time.

Community Harvesting Works!

In Warner Robbins, Georgia, Neal Edwards, a dynamic young pastor, has motivated most of his people to harvest all over town. What a joy it is to go back there and see what's happening.

In the north country, a circuit rider is doing the same thing. Daryl Witmer travels among three churches. I was overwhelmed when more than one hundred people showed up for a Harvesting Seminar in the rural town of Monson, Maine.

Yakima, Washington, is known for its great apples. Mark Snelling, a pastor in an old established church there, and I had very positive results equipping teams of people to harvest people rather than apples.

Pastor Vern Wilkinsins did an outstanding job of teaching his people the harvesting methods in a small but thriving mission church in Lakehead, California. He has since moved to Kansas and is doing the same thing there.

In Paso Robles, California, Pastor Red Ensley has trained more than one hundred people to harvest.

We have received letters from all over the country telling us harvesting works!

Is it any wonder that harvesters become so enthusiastic? They see God use them to accomplish miraculous things right before their eyes.

T·W·E·L·V·E

The Harvest Is Plentiful

We are ambassadors for Christ.
—2 Corinthians 5:20

What a joy it is to be with people who have just returned from having non-confrontive experiences in the harvest field. Each harvester attempts to express the sheer joy he feels after experiencing how the Holy Spirit has just worked to bring unsaved people to Jesus Christ. The harvester is unable to adequately express it.

Harvesting *is* overwhelming, indescribable and, in some respects, even more exciting than one's own conversion. And in addition to the great joy we experience in the here and now, we are promised eternal rewards. No wonder harvesting is an exhilarating experience.

I believe that being directly involved in the salvation of others is some of the gold, silver and precious stones that withstand the fire mentioned in 1 Corinthians 3:12-15. Only things that have eternal consequence will survive that test. As we let the Holy Spirit use us as harvesters for Jesus Christ, God promises us special rewards that not only start today but also last forever.

Is there anything more fulfilling and more reward-ing than introducing an individual to Jesus Christ and per-sonally witnessing the Holy Spirit give that individual eternal life? It follows then that there are blessings in equipping others to do harvesting. Teaching others how to harvest fulfills at least three direct commands:

- And He said unto them, "Go into all the world and preach the gospel to all creation" (Mark 16:15).
- Go therefore and make disciples of all the nations, bap-tizing them in the name of the Father and the Son and the Holy Spirit (Matthew 28:19).
- And the things which you have heard from me in the presence of many witnesses, these entrust to faithful men, who will be able to teach others also (2 Timothy 2:2).

So Close and Yet So Far

I am most enthusiastic and optimistic about the pos-sibilities for more major harvesting breakthroughs, but, as we come to the final pages of the book, I would be less than honest if I did not admit my frustration. Never have so many people known and experienced so much, yet fail to act.

We don't need to be reminded that we live in a sick society. As Christians we know that Jesus Christ alone of-fers the healing power that every person on earth desperately needs. But we behave as if the days of in-dividually talking to people about Jesus Christ are past. Have we convinced each other that with all the sophisti-cated developments in our society the world is just too advanced for anything so basic as asking questions about the gospel?

But that's the beauty of God's plan: It is really very simple. He wants His message to reach others through individuals like you and me. God has given us an important role in reconciling the lost. This is beautifully articulated in 2 Corinthians 5:18-20:

> Now all these things are from God, who reconciled us to Himself through Christ, and gave us the ministry of reconciliation, namely, that God was in Christ reconciling the world to Himself, not counting their trespasses against them, and He has committed to us the word of reconciliation. Therefore, we are ambassadors for Christ, as though God were entreating through us; we beg you on behalf of Christ, be reconciled to God.

D. L. Moody was not one to mince words. As active as he was in leading others to Christ, he included himself as part of the problem when he said, "We just don't believe in the lostness of the lost." Moody theorized that if God were to ask angel volunteers to come down to earth and live here for a lifetime just to lead one soul to Jesus Christ, every angel in heaven would jump at the chance because "there is no greater honor than to be an instrument in God's hands to lead one person out of the kingdom of Satan, into the glorious light of heaven." Oh, that we would catch a fraction of Moody's vision! *Nothing* is of more value than the eternal salvation of one soul. Do we *really* believe that in this generation?

Many years ago Hudson Taylor recognized that the main problem of evangelism is not the availability or receptivity of pre-Christians, but the reluctance of Christians. His words hit the target: "Over the centuries, our biggest problem has not been so much getting people to listen to the gospel as mobilizing believers to proclaim it."

Evangelism seems to be the most talked about and yet the most neglected ministry. You and I can change that if we will just start harvesting and encouraging others to do the same.

It has been said that God has no lips, no feet, no

hands—but ours. No doubt God could put the salvation message onto a giant television screen in the sky if He wanted to. But so far His plan is to use you and me. What a compliment that He wants our personal involvement in the most important job in the universe. God chose you and me to go to people who are out there in the everyday world.

The greatest part of Jesus' earthly ministry was hand-gathered. Probably all of the apostles were brought to Jesus by an individual who cared. No doubt some were confused or threatened by religious rules and regulations, like some of our neighbors. Maybe some were tired of pushy "religious" people, but were completely open to Jesus Christ. As we talk to our casual acquaintances, we can expect similar reactions. We can assume that many people have heard something of the gospel message and that they have all been exposed to "religious" people. Because of real or imagined bad experiences, many non-Christians are just not going to reach out to a church or seek to associate with "church" people. But this does not mean they are not ready to honestly answer our questions.

I appreciate Norman Geisler's confession of his disobedience to the Great Commission and willingness to share his experience. He was the director of a Christian youth organization for three years, a pastor for nine years and a Bible college professor for six years before he really started to talk to unbelievers one on one. He had never realized that people were not embarrassed to tell him how they felt about Jesus Christ. After learning to harvest, he said, "The most rewarding experiences I've had in my Christian life have not come from teaching, pastoring or ministering around the world. They come from meeting with non-Christians and seeing one after another come to know Christ." Oh, that we could all say the same thing!

As harvesters, we have learned how to approach our casual acquaintances in a non-threatening way by asking permission to ask questions. Instead of talking about our own experience, we simply let those who are ready make a commitment to Christ. We sensitively uncover why the non-Christian may not yet be ready and give him a chance to voluntarily come closer to Christ by looking at some easy-to-read material. We do not have to be ingenious, perfect or extremely knowledgeable.

It's almost too good to be true. We have a non-confrontive, practically foolproof way to find out where a person stands in relationship to Jesus Christ. Being a Christian is the greatest dimension of humanity. No true believer can ignore our Lord's command. We must help fulfill the Great Commission. Jesus' last command is our first concern.

We might be tempted to let His command overwhelm us, but 90 percenters take heart:

Come to Me, all who are weary and heavy-laden, and I will give you rest. Take My yoke upon you, and learn from Me, for I am gentle and humble in heart; and you shall find rest for your souls. *For My yoke is easy and My load is light* (Matthew 11:28-30).

To contact the author regarding evangelism training or Harvesting Seminars, write him at:

Harvesting Ministries
P. O. Box 205
11 Madrone Avenue
Mt. Hermon, CA 95041

Appendix A

Did Jesus Really Rise From the Dead?

Absolutely! There is no historical incident, no fact in history that has better evidence than the fact that Jesus Christ died and rose from the grave. Let's examine a few things about Him.

Everyone would probably agree that while He was here on earth, He lived the most influential life ever lived. After much reflection, one historian said, "Jesus is, in every respect, unique. Nothing can compare to Him. All history is incomprehensible without Christ."

Another amazing thing about Jesus is that He made outstanding claims about Himself. He made bold claims to deity. In effect, He said, "I AM GOD!" He pointed to the Old Testament prophecies. Things written hundreds of years before His coming were being fulfilled by Himself. He said He was the *only* source for forgiveness of sin. The *only* way of salvation.

The trial of Jesus was incredible. In most trials, people are tried for what they have done. Instead, Jesus was tried for what He *was*. He was convicted for His claims of supernatural power which were demonstrated and proven. On the very day of His crucifixion, the historical records indicate His enemies acknowledged He claimed to be God in the flesh.

After understanding these facts, we cannot say that Jesus was *just* a good moral man, an excellent teacher and perhaps even a prophet. Josh McDowell, in *More Than a Carpenter,* summarizes it like this: "You cannot put Him on the shelf as a great moral teacher. . . . He is either a liar, lunatic or Lord and God. You must make the choice."

All of this stands alongside the most important data, the bodily resurrection of Christ. Before His death, He repeatedly staked the truth of all His claims on the fact that He *would* rise from the dead.

The records show a series of appearances of Jesus *after* the resurrection. On one occasion, it involved more than 500 people. The disciples were understandably discouraged after the crucifixion, but after seeing Jesus, they took on an attitude of glorious certainty that He was indeed Lord God. In *Evidence That Demands a Verdict,* Josh McDowell says, "The most telling testimony of all is the lives of those early Christians. What caused them to go everywhere telling the message of the risen Christ? As a reward for their wholehearted allegiance to the 'risen Christ,' these early Christians were beaten, stoned, thrown to the lions, tortured and crucified. . . . yet they laid down their own lives as ultimate proof of their complete confidence in the truth of their message."

In spite of many adversities, the Christian movement *exploded* across the Roman Empire and beyond. The history of the whole first century would have been impossible without the resurrection. Clearly, the entire Christian faith rests upon the factually attested claim that death and sin have been conquered by the death and resurrection of Jesus. Happily, this claim can be investigated and examined by anyone willing to take the time to do so. In the meantime, God wants you to:

- Believe that Jesus Christ died and rose from the grave;
- Admit that you are a sinner;
- Agree to turn from your sin;
- Acknowledge Jesus Christ as Savior and Lord;
- Accept God's free gift of salvation.

Why Should I Acknowledge Jesus Christ as Savior and Lord?

The main purpose for Christ coming to earth was to keep you and me from being separated from God. The statement that Christ died for our sin is familiar to most of us. The study about why human sacrifice was necessary is extremely interesting but can get very deep. Most of us are satisfied with the explanation that God chose to accomplish His plan according to a sacrificial system that was well understood by the culture of that time. "But if God can do anything," someone might ask, "why didn't He just forgive our sins and let it go at that? Why was it necessary for Jesus to die on the cross?"

The simple explanation is that *all* sin is against God's divine law. Because He is completely righteous, He must penalize sin. Yet because He is completely merciful, He accepts the penalty for sin Himself. This is the way God chose to satisfy both His justice and His love.

In the person of Jesus Christ, He entered the world which He made. He identified Himself with man and his great need to be free of sin. In the darkness of those terrible hours on the cross, He took upon Himself the sin of the whole world. Only Jesus could do that. Why? Because He was 100 percent man, 100 percent sinless, 100 percent God. Because He was 100 percent man, He represented mankind. Because He was 100 percent sinless, He was the perfect sacrifice (which was required). Because He was 100 percent God, He was the only life that could be offered for the sins of *all* men for *all* time.

As Savior, Jesus wants to save you from your wrongdoings. Make no mistake about it: You and every other individual will eventually stand before God to give an account of how "perfect" you have been. You may be thinking, *I'll just go with what I've been. What I've done is good enough. I don't need any help.* The inescapable fact is that no one is good enough to overcome sin on his own. If you neglect or ignore the offer of so great a gift as salvation, the alternative is eternal separation from God. God is 100 percent holy and He cannot tolerate sin. If anyone refuses to accept His plan for cleansing, He will send them to a place of torment and everlasting separation. You cannot read the Bible and miss the references to hell. God's wrath is as much a part of the Bible as His perfect love.

What can you do? You must believe that Jesus died on the cross and rose from the grave, admit sin, agree to turn from sin and then willingly accept Jesus Christ not only as Savior but also as Lord. Actually the word *Lord* means ownership or absolute control, but as it applies to Jesus, it implies much more. Jesus has the divine title of *Lord God.* He is the creator, sustainer and supreme controller of the world. By His death and resurrection, He acquired a special ownership of you and mankind. So, as best you know how, you must turn your whole life over to Him. If you have not done so, God wants you to do it right now.

What are the results of this voluntary action? Immediately you will receive the free gift of eternal life. When you accept Jesus as Savior and Lord, He will put a new sense of purpose in your life. We all need the assurance that life has meaning. Lordship will help you realize personal fulfillment. Will you still have problems? Most certainly. But God will give you guidance to overcome your personal problems and use you to help others in a new and different way. He will also give you an inner peace and a sincere happiness deeper than anything you have ever experienced.

David tells us in Psalm 27: "The Lord is my light and my salvation." Is Jesus Christ not the brightest light in a dismal dark world? Isn't it best to follow the best light we know? You can bet your life on it.

Why Should I Admit Sin?

There are two facts about sin that are startling. The first is that mankind makes so little of it. Men love to joke about it, deny it and laugh at the "religious fanatics" who talk about it. The second fact is that God makes so much about sin. Sin is one of the central themes of the Bible and the reason Christ died and rose from the grave.

It is not surprising that people do not like to get serious about the subject. It is much easier to just avoid it. We hear them say things like, "Why talk about negative things like sin? Why not concentrate on positive things?" Well, of course it is nice to talk about pleasant things. It is certainly true that there is still much good done in the world.

We desperately want to convince ourselves that "sin" is just the problem of the *really* bad people. The criminal element and the abnormal misfits are the real problem. The popular philosophy of the world is that the human race is only a little twisted and that with steady, patient correction, we can remedy most of the bad in the world. How wrong this is. The greatest fallacy of the human race is that somehow man will create a heaven on earth. Our history books tell the story of our failure. Today's newspaper is a pathetic reminder of the nature of human nature. Our police departments tell us to double lock our doors and to stay off the streets. What's the problem?

When we look at humanity through the Bible microscope, it allows us to see the problem clearly. The problem is *me*. It is never a pleasant picture as the Lord Jesus points His X-ray at the heart of me, myself and I. The fifteenth chapter of Matthew says, "But the things that proceed out of the [my] mouth come from the heart, and those defile the man. For out of the [my] heart come evil thoughts." The Old Testament underlines this by saying, "Indeed, there is not a righteous man on earth who continually does good and never sins."

One philosopher said, "We must say of ourselves that we are evil, have been evil, and unhappily will be evil in the future. Nobody can deliver himself; someone must stretch out a hand and lift him up." Another said, "I don't know what the heart of a villain may be; I only know that of a virtuous man, and that is frightful."

"But wait a minute," we cry out. "I'm not all *that* bad. I don't do things to hurt people. I *try* to be a good person." Well, it is certainly true. There are a lot of "decent" people, both religious and otherwise, who are kind, neighborly and good citizens. The problem with the decent and indecent alike is that we are always *self-centered.* Any observant person will see this self-centeredness in himself and every other human being.

The thing that is wrong with humans is not just that some commit murder or adultery and steal, but that *all* of us are self-centered. The nice and the nasty, the religious person and the atheist all have the same disease—*self-centeredness.* If you are inclined to say, "Okay, but I don't sin," just think about your own self-centeredness. Compare what you say, think and do with what you know about Jesus. What the Bible says is true: "All have sinned and come short of the glory of God." What should I do about it? God wants you to honestly and sincerely:

- Believe that Jesus died for your sin and rose from the grave;
- Admit that you are a sinner;
- Agree to turn from your sin;
- Acknowledge Jesus Christ as your Savior and Lord;
- Accept God's free gift of salvation.

Why not get serious with God and do just that?

Why Should I Turn From Sin?

It has been well established that *everyone* is a sinner. Our society would like to believe that people are getting better and better, every day in every way, but God and everyone else knows that this is just not true.

After admitting that we are sinners, the next step is to honestly and sincerely agree to try to turn from sin. This is what the Bible calls *repentance*. In the past, there has been much misunderstanding about this word. *Repentance* is not grief or sorrow about wrongdoing, as many have come to believe. The true meaning of the word shows that it is a change of mind, a turning about and heading in another direction. Most religious groups will agree that it is wise to turn from sin. Christianity is different in that it asks that one willingly turn *from* sin *to* something, and that something is Jesus Christ *only*.

One might say, "Okay, Jesus Christ is who I must turn *to*, but what must I turn *from?*" Sorry, you won't find a list of don'ts here. All men and women have a moral sense. They know what the word *ought* means. *Ought* is never "I'd like to," or "Everyone else does it," or even "It might be a wise move to do it that way." The agreement about what is morally right transcends location, race and tribe. There is a moral order for mankind that is universally accepted. Mankind understands what "I ought" means.

Now, of course, it is true that moral sense requires some education. It is also true that the Judeo-Christian world relies on the Bible to determine what is morally right, but down deep inside each individual is a God-given conscience. You and I know what God does not like. *That is what He wants us to agree to turn away from.* That is what the Bible calls sin.

"How will I ever be able to do it?" you ask. Actually, you cannot without supernatural help: The next step is to acknowledge Jesus Christ as *Savior and Lord* of your life.

If you allow Jesus Christ to come in and take control of your life, He promises to make you a new person. He will give you the desire and power to do what you *ought*. He promised to help you turn away from the things you do not want to say, think or do. Your part is to voluntarily ask Him. God will keep His promise and take care of the rest. All you need to do is to be completely honest with Him. It is really very simple. God wants you to sincerely:

- Believe that Jesus Christ died and rose from the grave;
- Admit that you are a sinner;
- Agree to turn from your sin;
- Acknowledge Jesus Christ as your Savior and Lord;
- Accept God's free gift of salvation.

But the Bible also has a strong warning. Jesus wants to be Lord of your social, family and business life. He wants you to yield every aspect of your life to Him. He wants to have first place in *everything*. Do not try to do it part way. Do not try to give Him *some* of your sin and still hang on to some. Do not decide to live part of your life for Jesus and part according to your special desires. It does not work that way. Do not expect 500 percent awards for 50 percent surrender. He wants 100 percent surrender, but for it He rewards a thousandfold . . . forever.

Appendix B

Beginning Bible Study

This Bible study is based on the Gospel of John, the fourth book of the New Testament. This book presents *who Jesus Christ is* and *what He did* while He was on the earth. The word *gospel* means "good news."

The numbers at the end of each question indicate the location in the Gospel of John where the anwers may be found. For example: (3:16) indicates that the answer is found in John chapter 3, verse 16.

Some Helpful Definitions

Faith: believing that God will do what He says He will do.

Sin: any violation of God's standards of right and wrong.

Christian: one who believes that Jesus Christ died on the cross for sinners and was resurrected and has received Jesus Christ into his life as Savior and Lord.

1. Why was the Gospel of John written? (20:31)

_____

_____

_____

2. What three titles are given to Christ in John 14:6?

_____

_____

3. What kind of life did Christ come to give you? (10:10)

_____

4. What did God do for you that proves He loves you?
   (3:16)

_____

_____

5. What did Christ do for your sins? (1:29)

_____

_____

6. What must you do in order to become a child of God?
   (1:12)

_____

_____

7. Have you by faith invited Jesus Christ into your life?

_____

8. Did He come into your life when you asked Him?

_____

   Jesus said in Revelation 3:20: "Behold, I stand at
the door [of your life] and knock, if anyone hears My voice
and opens the door [receive Him], *I will come in.*"

   He promised to come in if you ask Him.

On the basis of the preceding verse, how do you know
that Christ is in your life?

_____

_____

9. What three things are true of you now that you have
   received Christ into your life? (5:24)

_____

_____

10. What did Jesus say about those who follow Him?
    (8:12)

_____

_____

11. Just before Christ left the earth, whom did He
    promise to send in His place? (14:26)

_____

12. Where did He say the Holy Spirit would dwell (live)?
    (14:16,17)

_____

_____

   After Christ died and rose from the grave, He went
to heaven and sent the Holy Spirit to live in all believers.
If you have received Christ, you have received the Holy
Spirit into your life. He is Christ's representative to us. He
and Christ are *One* as Jesus Christ and the Father are *One*
(John 14:9-12; 10:30; Romans 8:9).

13. What are six things that the Holy Spirit does? (7:37-39; 15:26; 16:7,8; 16:13-15)

_____

_____

_____

14. What illustration did Christ use to explain our relationship with Him? (15:15)

_____

_____

15. Why has Christ chosen you? (15:16)

_____

_____

16. After Andrew met Jesus personally, what did he want to do for his brother? (1:41,42)

_____

_____

For Further Study

Read the entire Gospel of John, at least one chapter a day. Write down a short title and brief summary for each chapter.

Appendix C

The
Harvesting Game

Preparation

One hundred and twenty slips of paper are needed for the game. Divide an 8-1/2" x 11" sheet of paper into twelve squares by drawing lines approximately 2-3/4" apart. Do this on both sides of ten separate sheets of paper (twelve boxes on each side).

Now type or print the word *Believe* in the center of each box on the front of two sheets. Do the same with the words *Admit, Agree, Acknowledge* and *Accept*. When you are finished you will have two sheets each with one of the five words in every box on the front.

On the back side of five different sheets, print the word *YES* in the center of nine boxes and the word *NO* in the center of the remaining three boxes.

On the back of the other five sheets, print the separate, individual stalls from the list that follows. Be careful to get the right ones on each sheet.

Believe

1. Just believing seems too easy.
2. Can you prove that Jesus Christ even existed?
3. I don't think anyone can be sure of that.
4. Isn't that pretty hard to believe?
5. Do you think Jesus Christ is the only way?
6. I'm a Catholic.
7. That's not what I was taught.

8. Do you have to believe in miracles?
9. Some say He did. Some say He didn't.
10. Why are you asking me that?
11. Most people don't care.
12. Aren't most people confused about that?

Admit

1. Well, I just do the best I can!
2. Actually, I'm a pretty good person.
3. Are you judging me?
4. What are some things you'd consider sins?
5. I don't want to go by someone else's rules.
6. Do you do things that are bad?
7. I think everyone should do what they want.
8. What do you mean by sin?
9. I'm not really that bad.
10. Isn't that a pretty personal question?
11. That's a tough question.
12. Don't you get in trouble when you ask that?

Agree

1. Forgive me, but I don't think that's your business.
2. What about all the hypocrites in the church?
3. We just need to be more loving.
4. Will I have to give up my night out?
5. Church people always seem so serious.
6. Why can't I do my own thing?
7. I'd like to, but I'll mess up.
8. Will I have to stop having fun?
9. I feel close to God when I'm fishing.
10. What do you mean by that?
11. I'm not really sure.
12. Why don't people just leave me alone?

Acknowledge

1. I wish religion wasn't so dogmatic.
2. Isn't the Bible full of errors?
3. I think Christianity is a psychological trip.
4. What do you think about TV preachers?
5. Christians don't have any fun.
6. Why can't I worship God on the golf course?
7. I don't like this born again stuff.
8. Are Buddhists going to Hell?
9. I think church is boring.
10. Why is God so narrow minded?
11. I'm all right the way I am.
12. Don't you think religious people are pushy?

Accept

1. I'm not sure there is a heaven.
2. Why does God allow cancer and AIDS?
3. I always thought good works would get me to heaven.
4. Are you sure there's life after death?
5. How much faith do you have to have?
6. I don't feel worthy.
7. I haven't thought much about it.
8. What does eternal life really mean?
9. There are so many churches.
10. Do you really think I'd make a good church member?
11. That's an interesting question.
12. How would you answer that?

Duplicate the ten sheets and keep the original for a master. Cut the slips along the lines you have drawn. When you are finished, you'll have nine "yes" cards, three "no" cards, and twelve different stall cards for each of the five words.

Each player will need three 3x5 cards: "A Sensitive Approach" (see *Figure B*), "God's Perfect Plan" (see *Figure C*) and "A Harvesting Guide" (see *Figure D*). We've found it helpful to color-code the cards: "A Sensitive Approach" is red; "God's Perfect Plan" is white; "A Harvesting Guide" is blue.

I'd suggest that before you begin to play you go around the table and have each player tell what their favorite dessert is. Notice the gestures, smiles and enthusiasm of everyone. Such animation needs to come through when talking about Jesus Christ as well.

How To Play

The game is played with four to eight players, comfortably seated around a table.

All 120 slips of paper are placed in the center of the table (with BAAAA words up) and thoroughly mixed.

Separate the twenty-four slips in a BAAAA category into four stacks of six slips and arrange on the table as illustrated in *Figure A.*

In the center of the table place a piece of paper with the letters "MJ" written on it. "MJ" is a hypothetical pre-Christian.

The object of the game is to give each player a chance to try to lead MJ to the Lord.

MJ, who is addressed as Mary, Joe, Mr. or Mrs. Jones, or simply MJ is very open to talk about spiritual things but at times quite unpredictable!

To begin the game, Player #1 asks the first question on the "A Sensitive Approach" card. The person to the left of Player #1 "responds" for MJ by reading the reply on the card word for word. Player #1 then asks the second question on the "A Sensitive Approach" card and the next player to the left replies, until the dialogue on the card is completed. *Players who are not the "harvester" will take turns in a clockwise direction answering for MJ.*

Player #1 then begins to ask the questions from the "God's Perfect Plan" card. MJ responds by turning up the first card in the stack which corresponds with the question being asked. For example, Player #1 asks, "Do you **believe** that Jesus Christ died for you on the cross and rose from the grave? (1 Corinthians 15:3,4)" MJ responds by turning over the first card in his or her "Believe" stack. This may be a yes, no or a stall. Player #1 then deals with the answer accordingly. The used slip is placed on the bottom of the pile.

When Player #1 receives a "No" response or if MJ makes a commitment, the interview is terminated and the next player starts by asking the first question on the "A Sensitive Approach" card. MJ responds starting from where the previous interview had left off.

Play continues until all have had at least one chance to be the harvester.

To Be Read at the Start of Each Game

The purpose of this exercise is to help harvesters *practice!*

Dealing with stalls and objections that come up unexpectedly is the best way to practice. Please do not improvise or try to ad lib. Reading each response word for word, and carefully following the instructions on the 3x5 cards, is the best way to help you and your fellow harvesters.

Please be careful not to get bogged down in unnecessary conversation, but as the game proceeds don't hesitate to stop to discuss different possibilities and outcomes for the harvesting experience. *Figure E* provides amplification of the BAAAA questions. *Figures F and G* offer some variations in answering stalls.

NOTE: There are three types of stalls that will come up when playing the game:

1. A basic stall—a typical question or comment.

2. A curve—an attempt to catch the Christian off guard.

3. A spacer—a disguised request for more time to think.

See if the group can identify these three types.

Layout for the Harvesting Game

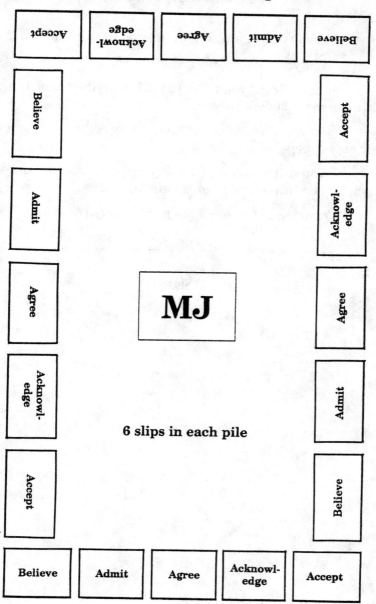

Figure A

A Sensitive Approach

As you may know, I'm interested in spiritual things.

Well yes, I know you go to church.

I don't want you to feel as if I'm trying to push my own personal beliefs on you.

I'm not worried about that, but of course, I do have my own beliefs.

Would it be okay if I ask you a few opinion questions? There are no right or wrong answers.

That's good. What's the first question?

Figure B
(One side only)

God's Perfect Plan

Do you . . .

- Believe Jesus Christ died for you on the cross and rose from the grave? (Jesus "rose" physically from the grave after three days.) (1 Corinthians 15:3,4)

- Admit you are a sinner? (Do you do things that God does not like?) (Romans 3:23)

- Agree to turn from sin to God? (Are you willing to turn away from the things that God does not like, as best you know how, right now?) (Acts 20:21)

- Acknowledge Jesus is Lord? (Are you willing to turn your life over to God and let Him run it?) (Romans 10:9)

- Accept God's free gift of salvation? (It's a free gift — no strings attached. You cannot "earn" it.) (Ephesians 2:8,9)

Will you say this simple prayer aloud?
Lord Jesus, I receive you as my Lord and personal Savior. Amen.

(Front)

If you honestly and sincerely said yes to those five questions and meant it in your heart (Romans 10:9) then you have the assurance of eternal life (1 John 5:11-13)!

Some Important Things for You to Do

1. Read your Bible to discover God's message for you (2 Timothy 3:15-17).

2. Talk to God in prayer often about yourself and others (Philippians 4:6,7).

3. Develop a lifestyle consistent with Bible principles (1 John 2:6).

4. Tell others about Christ in your own way (Acts 1:8).

5. Take the initiative to faithfully attend a Bible teaching church for worship, fellowship, growth and service (Hebrews 10:24,25).

(Back)

Figure C

Harvesting Guide

To Open: *"May we talk about spiritual things?"*

The Gospel: *Gently ask the five BAAAA questions. (Show them the card and read the questions aloud.)*

Handling an Objection:	*"If I could get you information that would help you convince yourself that (whatever the objection is), would you read it?"*

Then stop.

(Front)

Handling a Stall:	<u>Comment</u> — *"That's an interesting comment."* <u>Question</u> — *"I'm sorry, but I don't feel qualified to answer that question."* <u>Insistent</u> — *"Can we come back to that in just a moment?"*

Remember: *After every stall <u>don't stop</u>. Always go right back to BAAAA.*

Follow-up: *Carefully go over the back side of God's Perfect Plan.*

(Back)

Figure D

Simple Amplification of BAAAA

Believe: Jesus "rose" physically from the grave (after three days).

Admit: Do you do things that God does not like?

Agree: Are you willing to turn away from things that God does not like, as best you know how, right now?

Acknowledge: Are you willing to turn your life over to God and let Him run it?

Accept: It's a free gift — no strings attached. You cannot "earn" it.

Figure E

Variations on "I'm Not Qualified"

1. Yes. (If the stall is not controversial.)

2. No. (If the stall is not controversial.)

3. I don't know.

4. I'm not sure.

5. If you asked ten people that question, you would probably get ten different answers.

6. That's tough for me to explain.

7. I could tell you how I feel about that, but I'm really more interested in your opinion.

8. I wish I knew how to answer that!

9. Even theologians have a difficult time with that one.

10. That's a question that is almost impossible to answer.

Figure F

Variations on "That's Interesting"

1. Many say that.

2. Some say that.

3. I've never heard that before!

4. That's one way to look at it.

5. You may be right.

6. I appreciate your frankness.

7. Sounds like you've given that a lot of thought!

8. One of my best friends made that exact same comment.

9. You seem quite definite about that.

10. I'd love to explore that with you sometime.

Figure G

Appendix D

Let the Harvest Happen

By R. Michael Huber
Pastor, Pine Bluffs Baptist Church
Pine Bluffs, Wyoming

It all began at the Congress on Evangelism just before the BGC [Baptist General Conference] annual meeting in Portland, Oregon. I had seen and heard only half of Walter Bleecker's Harvesting Seminar when I realized that this approach to evangelism training would work in our community.

In my first two years pastoring in a small, rural Wyoming town, we had tried numerous ways to motivate people to share their faith in Christ. The results were always the same; those accustomed to witnessing witnessed, and the others didn't! Yet, the church leaders and I were convinced that the Lord Jesus intended for *every* believer to proclaim the good news.

Trained to Locate

Bleecker referred to this same dilemma: 90 percent (more like 98 percent) of the members of the average church have never had the thrill of personally leading someone to Christ. He affectionately called these the "90 percenters." Further, the Harvesting Seminar was specifically designed to train/equip these 90 percenters to "locate" those God had already prepared and prayerfully allow them to make a commitment to Jesus

Christ.

Now that was a switch! He wasn't even trying to train those who were already doing evangelism. He was just trying to get non-witnessing Christians involved in the natural sharing of the gospel with their acquaintances. They wouldn't have to become hard-sell, aggressive door-knockers. The purpose of the seminar was merely to help them discern whether these acquaintances had already been prepared by the Lord to respond to the message.

That took away most of the fear of evangelism.

With the approval of our church board, I proceeded to make arrangements for Mr. Bleecker to come to Pine Bluffs to present the three-hour Harvesting Seminar. I knew him to be a simple, lively man, with a dynamic enthusiasm about evangelism. I thought he would be received well. I was not disappointed.

Several other pastors wanted to participate as well. I presented the concept of the seminar to our sister BGC church in Albin, Wyoming, and at Frontier School of the Bible in La Grange. We planned to have lunch catered and charge only enough to cover the cost of materials, the meal and Walter's travel.

The deacons began praying for fifty or more from our own church to attend the seminar and thirty from other places. As it turned out, seventy-five people were there.

Green Fruit or Ripe?

The Harvesting Seminar is actually a combining of two concepts, each designed to make verbal witnessing as simple and non-threatening as possible. These two concepts are the "BAAAA" presentation and the "Stalls and Objections." These are clearly impressed upon conferees through entertaining lectures and small group exercises and discussions.

BAAAA, the sound a sheep makes, is "so appropriate for one who desires to be cradled in the arms of the Good Shepherd," as Walter comments. It is also an acrostic for a simplified (but not simplistic) presentation of the necessary truths of the gospel: "believe," "admit," "agree," "acknowledge" and "accept." These are printed on a 3x5 card for easy reference and use.

"Stalls and Objections" assists in discerning whether a person with whom the message is being shared is "green fruit" or "ripe." Has he been adequately prepared by the Holy Spirit to make a commitment to Jesus Christ, or is he still "on the way?"

Many people who are in fact ready to make a commitment still "stall" about making that decision. This should not prevent you from continuing to witness to these potential believers. On the other hand, an "objection" to one of the statements of the gospel represented by the BAAAA presentation indicates that this person is likely "green fruit" and you need not go on at this time.

Rather, change the subject and work on strengthening your relationship with the person. This sensitivity to what the Holy Spirit is doing in his life leaves him wide open for another evangelistic contact in the future. You have clarified the issues but have not "bruised the fruit."

The people were enthusiastic and anxious to try this sensitive and yet forthright approach with their friends and neighbors. Some had been seeking for years for a method of sharing the gospel with their neighbors. Now they believed it was possible. They found themselves saying, "Well, I can do that!"

In the two months following the seminar, we heard of more people witnessing and recorded more people making commitments to Christ than in the three years previous. This evangelism enthusiasm is continuing.

The Rest of the Story

However, the fruit born out of the Harvesting Seminar is less than half the story. We are seeing continuing results from the second part of Mr. Bleecker's training: The Community Harvesting Visitation Plan.

He had asked me to choose six people who were not in the habit of aggressively telling others of their faith in Christ to become our "pioneer team." We also sent introductory letters to people living near the church, telling them to expect a phone call from us. Then when he was here, Mr. Bleecker conducted some on-the-job training in "how to make evangelistic calls among our friends."

We phoned those people who had received the letters and we asked for appointments to visit. We simply wanted to become better acquainted with our neighbors, we told them.

This proved to be a worthwhile approach, for some very

"green fruit" was discovered. We didn't spend a lot of time and effort knocking on doors and meeting with cold receptions. We visited only those who knew we were coming and, in fact, had invited us. After a time of warm conversation we shared a pre-planned presentation of the gospel.

A Delightful Side-Benefit

It is important to realize that this community harvesting approach is not primarily a visitation evangelism program. Rather, it is an arena in which to train 90 percenters to share their faith and to discern the differences between "stalls" and "objections." Once they become familiar with a few simple "how-to's" and experience the joy of talking about spiritual things, they recognize and capitalize on evangelistic opportunities much more frequently.

Of course, one of the delightful side-benefits is that we actually are seeing people make commitments to Christ — while we ourselves are being trained.

When a pioneer team member has been trained, he or she in turn takes on the equipping of another 90 percenter and another and another. And so our weekend Harvesting Seminar led to the on-going community harvesting, through which on-the-job discipleship in evangelism is taking place in the church. God has used Walter Bleecker and the Harvesting Seminar to turn us around. God is working and changing lives, and *we* are a part of it.

This article originally appeared in the Baptist General Conference's *The Standard* (January 1986), pp. 22-24, and is reprinted with permission.